e|Merg

Developing Youth as Fully Devoted Disciples

Director's Book

07 08 09 10 11 12 13 14 15 16—10 9 8 7 6 5 4 3 2 1

Cover Design: Keely Moore

Contents

What Is E|MERGE?

E|MERGE is a comprehensive resource for youth group programming.

Being a youth minister is a demanding job, regardless of whether you are full time or part time, paid staff or unpaid servant leader. Preparing elaborate evening programs that are fun, educational, and transformational can be extremely challenging, especially when free time is scarce. Chances are that you didn't get into student ministry because you love to create PowerPoint® presentations or read how-to manuals about video-editing software. No, you love being with students, and E|MERGE aims to give you more of what you love by giving you lesson plans, games, handouts, and multimedia resources that will make your preparation much easier.

The E|MERGE Model

The E|MERGE model of youth group programming combines engaging large-group teaching and meaningful small-group experience.

1. **Engaging large-group teaching:** This portion of the program brings all of your youth together for games and a message. Game ideas and message content are found in this book, and a PowerPoint® show that goes along with each talk is included on the DVD. Some sessions also have a short video segment, also included on the DVD.

2. **Meaningful small-group experience:** The energy of the large-group teaching is balanced by the intimacy of small groups. A small group consists of five to ten youth who are close in age and an adult leader. The small-group setting gives youth a chance to go deeper into each session's topic through activities, discussion, and Bible study. As the youth in each cluster grow in their relationships with one another, they will also grow closer to God.

Both the large-group teaching and the small-group gathering are meant to last between forty-five minutes and an hour, depending on how much time you spend on housekeeping and announcements. Beginning with the large-group teaching then proceeding with the small groups is best. But if need dictates, the small groups can meet prior to the large-group gathering. The best option for some leaders may be to have some small groups to work beforehand and others meet afterward.

Caution: You Can't Do This Alone

You cannot do any of these sessions by yourself. For effective programming, you need help from other adults from your congregation who have been called by God to minister to youth. The "called by God" part is important. Don't look for just adults who are willing, and don't fall into the trap of enlisting adults who seem "cool." You need members of the congregations who have a gift for working with adolescents.

If God has already sent you some gifted adults who can help you make these programs a success, great! If not, get up in front of your congregation and ask everyone to pray about whether God has called and equipped them to help with the youth ministry. Talk to groups in your church that have completed a spiritual-gifts inventory, and find out whether anyone discovered that he or she has a gift for teaching or working with teenagers. And ask your students to suggest adults; you may be surprised by what names come up.

For the programs included in this resource, your adult volunteers will serve as small-group leaders. The small-group leader's guides included in the E|MERGE box help your these adults better understand their role in your youth ministry and equip them to facilitate each of the thirteen small-group sessions. Each of these books include a CD-ROM that features audio tracks about the leaders' role in your ministry, as well as tips for working with youth in a small-group setting.

The Small-Group Experience

All Christians benefit from being part of a small group of people who are bound by love, trust, and respect. Youth benefit most from being in a group made up of people their age. Since younger (middle school) youth and older (high school) youth are at different stages of physical and mental development, you should divide your students into small groups based on age. If you have eight youth, five of whom are in middle school and three of whom are in high school, create one small group with the middle school youth and one with the high school youth. If you have thirty youth, you might be able to create groups of just middle school boys or middle school girls. If you have eighty students, you might have the luxury of assigning groups based on grade level and sex (such as seventh-grade boys and seventh-grade girls).

Regardless of how many youth are in your ministry, giving your students time in a small group with other youth their age is important. For that reason, this resource comes with two leader's guides for adult volunteers who will be leading small groups—one for a leader working with older youth and one for a leader working with younger youth.

The e|Merge DVD

The DVD included in this resource provides you with a wealth of materials that you will need for your programming:

- **Message Maps:** Each of the thirteen programs has a Message Map. These printable PDFs provide key teaching points, Scriptures, and questions for written reflection and discussion. Each youth will need a copy of the Message Map during the large-group time.

- **PowerPoint® slideshows:** These slideshows give you a striking visual aid to enhance each large-group teaching. The DVD also contains JPG files of every PowerPoint® slide that you can use to create your own visual aids if you so choose. Three sessions also have PowerPoint® games, fun quizzes that you can use as opening activities.

- **Movies:** Seven of the thirteen programs have short video segments that illustrate the key teaching points. And the units "Room Raiders" and "The Call" come with a short "bumper" that you can use to introduce all of the sessions in that unit. You can access these videos and bumpers by inserting the DVD into a standard DVD player. You can download MPEG, QuickTime, and Windows Media® versions of the movies by placing the DVD in your computer.

- **Small-group handouts:** The DVD also gives you all of the handouts that will be used in the small-group sessions. Your adult leaders can access these handouts on the CDs included in their leaders' guides. But the PDFs are also available on the DVD so that you can keep tabs on what the small groups are talking about.

How to Use This Book

This book and accompanying DVD give you lesson plans, handouts, key Scriptures, and discussion questions for thirteen one-hour sessions with your large group. You will find at the beginning of each session plan "The Big Idea" (the key teaching for that session), "Session Texts" (the key Scriptures for that session), and "Before You Teach This Lesson" (something for you to reflect on as you prepare for the session).

Each lesson plan then includes the following:

• **Warm-Up:** opening activities related to the key teaching for that session.

• **Teaching:** a talk that you will deliver to the large group. This book provides word-for-word content for each talk that you can adapt and customize as you see fit.

You can enhance the teaching by using the Message Maps, PowerPoint® shows, and video segments found on the DVD. The teaching in each session ends with a suggestion for a closing prayer.

The teaching sections provide cues for changing the PowerPoint® slides. For example, *PPT 3* means, "the third slide in the PowerPoint® presentation," and *PPT 4* means, "the fourth slide."

PowerPoint® Teaching Cues

The teaching sections provide cues for changing the PowerPoint® slides. For example, *PPT 3* means, "the third slide in the PowerPoint® presentation," and *PPT 4* means, "the fourth slide."

Unit 1: Glow

"Glow" is a three-session unit that focuses on spiritual practices and time with God. While E|MERGE is for evening youth-group programs, we must talk to youth about how they connect with God and mature in faith when they are away from church.

This unit encourages students to set aside time daily for prayer, Scripture and devotional reading, and reflection. The three sessions are called "Hanging Out With God," "Prayer," and "The Word."

Hanging Out With God

The first session, "Hanging Out With God," challenges youth to make time each day for prayer and devotion and find a space where they can be alone with God.

This session features the video "On Campus—Connecting With God" (on the DVD).

Prayer

As the title suggests, the second session is all about prayer. Youth will learn that prayer is nothing more than a conversation with God and that, as with any conversation, listening is as important as talking.

This session features the video "On Campus—Prayer" (on the DVD).

The Word

The final session in "Glow" looks at the Bible and the importance of regularly reading and studying God's word.

This session features the video "On Campus—The Bible" (on the DVD).

Glow: Hanging Out With God

The Big Idea

Youth need to find a time and a place in which they can "get real" with God. When they consistently hang out with God, they will glow with the Holy Spirit; God's heart will become their heart, and they will receive God's wisdom.

Session Texts

- **Exodus 34:28-35** (*Message*): Moses was there with God forty days and forty nights. He didn't eat any food; he didn't drink any water. And he wrote on the tablets the words of the covenant, the Ten Words.

  When Moses came down from Mount Sinai carrying the two Tablets of The Testimony, he didn't know that the skin of his face glowed because he had been speaking with God. Aaron and all the Israelites saw Moses, saw his radiant face, and held back, afraid to get close to him.

  Moses called out to them. Aaron and the leaders in the community came back and Moses talked with them. Later all the Israelites came up to him and he passed on the commands, everything that God had told him on Mount Sinai.

  When Moses finished speaking with them, he put a veil over his face, but when he went into the presence of God to speak with [the Lord], [Moses] removed the veil until he came out. When he came out and told the Israelites what he had been commanded, they would see Moses' face, its skin glowing, and then he would again put the veil on his face until he went back in to speak with God.

- **Matthew 6:6** (*Message*): "Here's what I want you to do: Find a quiet, secluded place so you won't be tempted to role-play before God. Just be there as simply and honestly as you can manage. The focus will shift from you to God, and you will begin to sense [God's] grace."

- **Mark 1:35**: In the morning, while it was still very dark, [Jesus] got up and went out to a deserted place, and there he prayed.

Before You Teach This Lesson

Exodus tells us that after spending forty days with God, Moses returned to the Israelites with a holy sunburn. His face glowed because he had been in God's presence. When we have done so, our lives will reflect the character of God. We cannot help but reflect the presence of God on our faces.

We cannot expect to take students to a place where we have not been ourselves. All leadership begins with self-leadership. Are you creating space in your life for God to speak to you? Do you model the importance of time with God on a daily basis?

From the Writer

I am a little embarrassed to admit this shortcoming, but time with God every day didn't become an important part of my spiritual journey until four years ago. As a professional minister, I loved God. I prayed, read Scripture, and fasted on occasions. But I was not practicing life-transforming spiritual disciplines.

I remember when my college rugby coach, Nigel, pulled me aside at practice one day. He said something to the effect of: "Mr. Milthaler, you're out of shape. We get only two hours of practice a day; and I need to use that time for technique, not getting your rear into shape. You need to learn to do that on your own." I needed to make physical conditioning part of my daily life. The next day, I started an exercise routine that got me better prepared to play the game.

In recent years, *spiritual* conditioning has become a vital part of my life. I spend time reading Scripture, writing in my journal, and praying. Conditioning gives me focus, direction, and clarity for my God-mission. Just as working out improves my physical endurance, time with God every day improves my spiritual endurance.

Music Option:
"Spending Time With You" by Stellar Kart (*All Gas. No Brake.*)

Think through the following questions to prepare yourself for teaching this lesson:

• How much ease do you have making time for God every day? What makes it difficult? What makes it easy?

• Can you describe in one sentence why time with God should be a priority for teenagers?

• What would happen if your students intentionally spent time with God every day for one month? What would be different about your group? How would they act towards one another, their families, and people who don't know God?

Warm-up

What You'll Need
skateboard, four 9" to 18" traffic cones (or four chairs) for every four to ten youth

Option 1: Skateboard Relay

Beforehand, create obstacle courses of traffic cones (or chairs). For each team of four to ten youth, place four cones a few feet apart in a straight line.

Divide students into teams of four to ten. Give each team a skateboard, and line up each team in front of a line of cones. Have the teams do a relay race in which each person skates, weaving through the cones to the end of the line and back. The first team for which every person completes the course is the winner.

To make this game interesting, give the following instructions for each leg:

• Sit on the board.
• Lie on your stomach.
• Go on the board two at a time.

• Sit backwards.
• Lie on your back.
• Stand backwards.

What You'll Need
skateboard, helmet, plastic bowling pins (or objects such as small trashcans and cardboard tubes)

Option 2: Human Bowling

In your meeting space or in a hallway, mark off a space about forty feet long. (If you are on carpet, shorten the length.)

12

Use tape to create a foul line at one end of the lane; set up ten bowling pins (in standard formation) at the opposite end.

Have each team select one member to lie on his or her stomach on the skateboard. The human bowling balls must keep their hands at their sides and may not use their arms or legs to knock over the pins. The teams must push the person on the skateboard toward the pins to knock over as many as possible. Keep score as you would in a traditional game of bowling; determine beforehand how many frames you will play.

Each time a team bowls, have a different member act as a bowling ball; make sure that every person who is sent crashing into the pins is wearing a helmet.

Option 3: Skateboarding Demo

Invite a skilled skateboarder to do a demonstration for your students. They may know of such a person, or one of them might be experienced enough to pull it off.

Video: On Campus—Connecting With God

What You'll Need
"On Campus—Connecting With God" video from the DVD, DVD player or computer and projector

Show the video entitled "On Campus—Connecting With God" from the DVD; then have the youth get into groups of four to five to discuss these questions:

• Which of the college students interviewed in this video do you most relate to? Why?

• Which of these students can you not relate to at all? Why?

• What spiritual practices do the students in this video name? What are some spiritual disciplines that they did not name?

• Which spiritual disciplines are named by the most students in the video? Which practices seem to have the biggest impact on their lives?

Teaching

Give this talk to the large group; or put it in your own words, using the key Scriptures and your own illustrations. Begin by updating the youth on what's going on in your youth ministry (PPT 2).

Let's say that one day you decide you want to learn how to skateboard (PPT 3). You go to your local skate shop and buy the coolest board you can find, with state-of-the-art trucks and wheels; to be safe, you get a helmet and knee and elbow pads. And while you're there, you get a pair of shoes and a new hoodie so that you can look the part.

Then you go down to your local skate park and start hanging out with people who know how to skate. At first, you learn the basics. Staying on the board without falling off is a major accomplishment. A few weeks later, you learn how to ollie (a jump performed without using the hands or any accessories); then you begin on the small ramps. After a few months, you're a decent skater. Hanging out with skaters has paid off.

The next part of this scenario is a little out there; but let's say that one day, professional skater Tony Hawk comes through your town and stops by the skate park. He sees you skate and pulls you aside. Tony says to you, "I've been watching you out there, and it looks like you have some natural talent. If you're willing, I'd love to teach you how to skate like a pro. If you meet me here every day for an hour, I'll teach you how to skate like I do."

You decide that you would be crazy if you didn't do whatever it takes to meet Tony Hawk every day. You learn from a master, someone who knows skateboarding inside and out. Over time, Tony's style and technique rub off on you.

Before long, your life is totally different. You're skating at competitions all over the country and winning medals and prize money. People, not knowing that Tony Hawk taught you, are comparing your styles. They're saying, "That looks just like Tony Hawk—there's something Hawkish about the kid's skating."

You can apply a similar illustration to hanging out with Jesus. Imagine that Jesus came along and invited you to spend an hour, half-hour, or even fifteen minutes a day with him. Over time, you'd talk and act more like Jesus. But while the Tony Hawk story is a fantasy, the Jesus story is real. The Savior *does* want to spend time with you every day; and if you accept his invitation, your life will never be the same.

The series we're starting this week is called "Glow," and the key Scripture is from **Exodus 34:28-35.** Moses was on the mountain where God had given him the Ten Commandments. Let's pick up at the point when Moses was coming back down to the people (PPT 4).

Here *The Message*'s paraphrase of the Scripture:

> Moses was there with God forty days and forty nights. He didn't eat any food; he didn't drink any water. And he wrote on the tablets the words of the covenant, the Ten Words (PPT 5).
>
> When Moses came down from Mount Sinai carrying the two Tablets of The Testimony, he didn't know that the skin of his face glowed because he had been speaking with God. Aaron and all the Israelites saw Moses, saw his radiant face, and held back, afraid to get close to him.
>
> Moses called out to them (PPT 6). Aaron and the leaders in the community came back and Moses talked with them. Later all the Israelites came up to him and he passed on the commands, everything that God had told him on Mount Sinai.
>
> When Moses finished speaking with them, he put a veil over his face (PPT 7), but when he went into the presence of God to speak with [the Lord], [Moses] removed the veil until he came out. When he came out and told the Israelites what he had been commanded, they would see Moses' face, its skin glowing (PPT 8), and then he would again put the veil on his face until he went back in to speak with God.

Have you ever had a sunburn? I'm talking about the kind that itches and hurts for a week. Have you ever had raccoon eyes because you were wearing sunglasses at the beach? A sunburn is proof that you've been in the sun. The effect is evident to you and everyone who sees you.

Moses came off the mountain with a holy sunburn. He had spent forty days with God, and that experience showed on his face. Moses glowed so much that the people had to cover up his face because they were afraid of him. I think that as followers of Christ, we should have a glow about ourselves because we are hanging out with God (PPT 9).

Mark 1:35 tells us that even Jesus, God incarnate, spent time with his heavenly Father. The verse says, "In the morning, while it was still very dark, [Jesus] got up and went out to a deserted place, and there he prayed" (PPT 10).

Jesus tells us to do the same. In **Matthew 6:6** he says:

> "Here's what I want you to do: Find a quiet, secluded place so you won't be tempted to role-play before God. Just be there as simply and honestly as you can manage. The focus will shift from you to God, and you will begin to sense [God's] grace" (*Message*).

We first need to set aside time (PPT 11). Many of us need to make time in our schedule for something if we want it to happen. Some people prefer to be with God first thing in the morning; others favor prayer and devotion right before bed. The time of day isn't what's important. What *is* essential is that you make time. What time of day is best for you? Fill in this time on your Message Map.

Give the youth a minute to answer the question about time of day on their Message Map.

The second blank in your Message Map asks you to think of a place where you can be alone with God (PPT 12). Having a place is important for maximizing this special time. **Matthew 6:6** mentions a quiet, secluded spot. Not everyone prefers silence; some people connect with God more readily while music is playing. And people prefer different levels of lighting. The important thing is to eliminate distractions. Turn off the television, turn off the phone, and remove anything else that might lead your mind astray. Some people have one place where they spend their daily devotional time; others have multiple places. On your Message Map, write two or three places where you could spend time alone with God.

Give the youth a minute to answer the question about a place where they can spend time with God on their Message Map.

In the coming weeks, I want you to select a daily devotional resource, a time each day to spend with God, and a place (or places) where you can be alone with God. I can help you find devotional books, magazines, or websites that are a good fit for you. So can your small-group leaders. Each of you will have a different devotional experience. Some of you may already faithfully spend time every day with God. Others of you will struggle to get into a routine. Some of you can sit in silence for a half-hour, praying and meditating. Others of you will need a written reflection or prayer to keep you focused (PPT 13).

Hanging out at a skate park once a week will help you learn how to board. Time with a professional every day will help you more. After a while, you will mimic the professional's style and technique. The same is true for coming to youth group and worship. These weekly gatherings are important, but your relationship with God will grow much stronger when you spend time daily with Christ.

Let's pray.

> Gracious God, thank you for loving us and being present with us and forgive us for not hanging out with you as much as we should. Help us make spending time for prayer and devotion a priority. We pray these things in the name of your son, Jesus Christ.

Glow: Prayer

The Big Idea

Prayer is simply a conversation with God. The elegance of our words doesn't matter as much as our attitude and the orientation of our hearts. Prayer is as much about listening to God as it is talking to God. Jesus gave us an example of how to pray: the Lord's Prayer.

Session Texts

- **Exodus 34:28-35** (*Message*): Moses was there with God forty days and forty nights. He didn't eat any food; he didn't drink any water. And he wrote on the tablets the words of the covenant, the Ten Words.

  When Moses came down from Mount Sinai carrying the two Tablets of The Testimony, he didn't know that the skin of his face glowed because he had been speaking with God. Aaron and all the Israelites saw Moses, saw his radiant face, and held back, afraid to get close to him.

  Moses called out to them. Aaron and the leaders in the community came back and Moses talked with them. Later all the Israelites came up to him and he passed on the commands, everything that God had told him on Mount Sinai.

  When Moses finished speaking with them, he put a veil over his face, but when he went into the presence of God to speak with [the Lord], he removed the veil until he came out. When he came out and told the Israelites what he had been commanded, they would see Moses' face, its skin glowing, and then he would again put the veil on his face until he went back in to speak with God.

- **Job 12:13** (*Message*): "True wisdom and real power belong to God; from him we learn how to live, and also what to live for."

- **Matthew 6:6** (*Message*): "Here's what I want you to do: Find a quiet, secluded place so you won't be tempted to role-play before God. Just be there as simply and honestly as you can manage. The focus will shift from you to God, and you will begin to sense [God's] grace."

- **1 John 1:9** (NRSV): If we confess our sins, he who is faithful and just will forgive us our sins and cleanse us from all unrighteousness.

From the Writer

When I was a child, I would often spend nights with my grandfather. At bedtime he would always ask me which one of us was going to pray first. I always wanted to go first, because Grandpa's prayers would last "about an hour" and I would usually fall asleep before he said, "Amen." I can still remember the passion with which he prayed. His words weren't big, and he hadn't written an elegant Shakespearian sonnet for God. His prayers were plain, simple, sincere, and beautiful.

Before You Teach This Lesson

As Christians, prayer surrounds us. Most church meetings don't formally start until the group has prayed and asked for God's guidance. Just about every worship service includes corporate prayer; most include several. Prayer is also a staple at Christian concerts, retreats, service projects, and outings. While praying together with our brothers and sisters in Christ is important, corporate prayer alone is not sufficient. God desires to hear from us in personal and intimate ways. Prayer re-aligns the focus in our lives, shifting it from ourselves to God.

How is your prayer life? Reflect on the following questions as you prepare to teach this lesson:

• How intimate is your prayer life? How often do you spend time alone with God?

• How fresh is your prayer life? Do your prayers ever seem stale or recycled? How do you keep your prayers fresh?

• How effectively do you focus on God during your prayers? Do you often find your mind wandering?

• How balanced are your prayers? Do you have a conversation with God in which you actively listen, or do you do all the talking?

• If you had one hour to communicate biblical and theological truth about prayer to your students, what would you say and do?

Warm-up

Option 1: SPAMMED

Divide the students into groups of four or five; ask them to answer the following trivia questions about SPAM:

1. **T**/F SPAM is a syllabic abbreviation for "SPiced hAM."

2. **T**/F It's believed that Senator Robert Byrd used to eat sandwiches of SPAM, mayonnaise, and white bread three times a week.

3. T/**F** SPAM was created during the Space Race and originally eaten by astronauts.

4. How many millions of cans of SPAM are sold worldwide each year?
   A. 126 million
   B. 134 million
   C. 141 million
   D. 152 million

5. **T**/F Soviet leader Nikita Krushchev once credited SPAM with the survival of the WWII Russian army.

6. Which is not an ingredient in SPAM?
   A. Chopped pork shoulder meat with ham meat added
   B. Beet extract
   C. Salt
   D. Sugar
   E. Sodium nitrite

7. How long do SPAM's makers say a vacuum-sealed can of it lasts?
   A. 5 years
   B. 15 years
   C. 25 years
   D. 50 years
   E. Forever

Tie breaker: Where is the official SPAM Museum located?

A. Austin, Minnesota
B. Hormel, Kansas
C. Gatlinburg, Tennessee
D. Sioux Falls, South Dakota

Option 2: I've Done It!

If you have twenty or more youth, divide them into groups of ten to fifteen. The objective of the game is for everyone in the group to state something that he or she has done that no one else in the group has done. Think of a clever way to decide who will start the game (such as choosing the person with the longest eyelashes or the person with the most colorful shoes).

Going clockwise around the circle, have the rest of the teens say what they've done. If a student names something that one of his or her classmates has done, that person must go again until he or she comes up with something that no one else has done.

Video: On Campus—Prayer

Show the video "On Campus—Prayer" from the DVD; then have the youth divide into groups of four to five to discuss these questions:

> **What You'll Need**
> "On Campus—Prayer" video from the DVD, DVD player or computer and projector

• Which of the college students interviewed in this video do you most relate to? Why?

• Which of these students can you not relate to at all? Why?

• More than one of the students said that they prayed when they needed something or when times were rough. Why is praying during the good times important too?

• If someone were to ask you why praying regularly is important, how would you answer?

What You'll Need
"Glow: Prayer"
PowerPoint® show and
Message Map (from the
DVD), a few week's worth
of your junk mail

Teaching

Give this talk to the large group; or put it in your own words, using the key Scriptures and your own illustrations. Begin by updating the youth on what's going on in your youth ministry (PPT 2).

For the opening illustration, present your junk mail (PPT 3).

Have you ever received junk mail? How about SPAM e-mail? Here's some of the junk mail that I've received in the last few weeks.

Read some of the phrases that appear on your junk mail, such as "current resident," "you may have won $1 million," "meet singles in your area," and "you've been pre-approved."

Many households receive more junk mail than important mail. Thousands of trees are cut down each year so that we can have full mailboxes. Usually it's the same stuff: credit-card offers, coupons you'll never use, magazine subscription offers, and catalogs you don't look at. Opening a real letter from a real person has become a rare treat.

Junk mail and SPAM annoy us because they are impersonal (PPT 4). These messages come from organizations or companies that don't seem to know us or care about us; they just want something from us—usually our money. Today we're going to talk about the junk mail and SPAM that we send to God. We're going to talk about praying in a way that is personal and sincere.

Last time, we began this series, which is called "Glow" (PPT 5). The name comes from **Exodus 34,** which says, "When Moses came down from Mount Sinai carrying the two Tablets of The Testimony, he didn't know that the skin of his face glowed because he had been speaking with God" (*Message*). You'll recall from last time that Moses spent forty days and nights on the mountain with God (PPT 6). When he came back down to his people, he had a holy sunburn.

When we hang out with God, we glow; we cannot help but be changed by God's power and presence. In our last session, we talked about the importance of time with God every day—scheduling a time, picking a place, and getting real with God. This time, we're going to focus on prayer and the impact it can have on our lives (PPT 7).

The first thing we need to realize about prayer is that prayer is simply a conversation with God. This idea may sound like a no-brainer, but too often we don't approach prayer from this perspective. Maybe we see it as a formality or an obligation. Maybe we focus so much on our posture, the structure of our prayer, and the words we use that we don't allow ourselves just to talk with God. We need to take seriously any conversation with the Creator of the universe, but we should also remember that the Lord truly loves us and wants to chat with us.

When you keep in mind that prayer is simply a conversation with God, you free yourself to pray open, honest, and beautiful prayers, even if they don't include words such as *thou, beseech,* and *art* (PPT 8). Listen to what Jesus says in this translation of **Matthew 6:6** from *The Message:*

> "Here's what I want you to do: Find a quiet, secluded place so you won't be tempted to role-play before God. Just be there as simply and honestly as you can manage. The focus will shift from you to God, and you will begin to sense [God's] grace."

Praying aloud, even when you are alone, may help you stay focused and truly have a conversation with God. When you use actual words, instead of just thoughts, you can better concentrate on what you want to say to God and you are less likely ramble. Jesus, in **Matthew 6:7,** tells us that we should not "heap up empty phrases" in our prayers. Instead, we need to be straight with God and say what's in our hearts.

If you feel like you need help praying, you're in good company. Even Jesus' disciples asked him how they should pray (PPT 9). Jesus told them:

> "When you pray, say:
>   Father, hallowed be your name.
>   Your kingdom come.
>   Give us each day our daily bread.
>   And forgive us our sins,
>   for we ourselves forgive everyone indebted to us.
>   And do not bring us to the time of trial."
> **(Luke 11:2-4)**

Invite the youth to recite the version of the Lord's Prayer that your congregation says in worship.

On your Message Map, underline the Lord's Prayer as I read it until I tell you to stop. "Our Father, who art in heaven, hallowed be thy name. Thy kingdom come, thy will be done on earth as it is in heaven." Stop (PPT 10). The opening lines that you just underlined show us that we should put God's plans before our plans. Too often, we just go to God with a list of our needs and wants without thinking about what God needs and wants. But our prayers should acknowledge God's greatness, thank the Lord for all that God has done, and ask about the Lord's will for our lives.

Now underline the next sentence, "Give us this day our daily bread" (PPT 11). Jesus recognized that God is the source for all our needs. "Daily bread" refers to food but also our other basic needs—physical, emotional, and spiritual. When we talk to God about our needs, we should acknowledge that God is the one who meets our needs.

Underline the next sentence, "And forgive us our trespasses, as we forgive those who trespass against us" (PPT 12). Jesus tells us to own up to our mistakes. No matter how ashamed we are of what we have done, we need to tell God about it (PPT 13). According to **1 John 1:9,** "If we confess our sins, [God] who is faithful and just will forgive us our sins and cleanse us from all unrighteousness." Sin has a way of separating us from God. Confessing our mistakes draws us back to God.

Finally, underline the rest of the prayer: "And lead us not into temptation, but deliver us from evil. For thine is the kingdom, and the power, and the glory forever. Amen." Jesus acknowledged that God is the source of our power (PPT 14). The only way to deal with life's pressures is to rely on God's strength and power. Alone, we can do nothing (PPT 15). **Job 12:13** in *The Message* says, "True wisdom and power belong to God; from him we learn how to live, and also what to live for."

With the Lord's Prayer, Jesus teaches us what to say when we pray; but prayer is as much about listening as it is about talking (PPT 16). Most of the prayers we say together in worship, in youth group, and at other gatherings involve talking—we recite a prayer together or

e|Merge 1.0: Director's Guide

one person does the talking for us. This style of prayer is good, but we also need prayer time when we can just be quiet and listen.

Do any of you have friends who talk too much? Do you ever just want to scream, "HOW ABOUT ASKING ME WHAT *I* THINK? I'VE BEEN LISTENING TO YOU FOR AN HOUR, AND IT DOESN'T APPEAR THAT YOU ARE ANYWHERE CLOSE TO STOPPING!"? God is too gracious to blow up at us like that, but if we don't listen, we won't hear God's instructions for our lives. If we, as the Lord's children, are to accomplish God's purpose in the world, we need to listen.

Let's review:

- Prayer is simply a conversation with God (PPT 7).
- We should put God's plans above our plans (PPT 10).
- God is the source of all of our needs (PPT 11).
- We should own up to our mistakes (PPT 12).
- God is the source of our power (PPT 14).
- Prayer is as much about listening as it is about talking (PPT 16).

To close, let's pray together the Lord's Prayer.

Glow: The Word

The Big Idea

God's Word is more than a collection of stories; it shows the Lord's interaction with God's people over time. This story continues and offers guidance for living, as well as transformation.

Session Texts

• **Psalm 119:9** (*Message*): How can a young person live a clean life? By carefully reading the map of your Word.

• **Psalm 145:13** (NRSV): Your kingdom is an everlasting kingdom, and your dominion endures throughout all generations. The Lord is faithful in all [God's] words, and gracious in all [God's] deeds.

• **Matthew 7:24-27** (NRSV): "Everyone then who hears these words of mine and acts on them will be like a wise man who built his house on rock. The rain fell, the floods came, and the winds blew and beat on that house, but it did not fall, because it had been founded on rock. And everyone who hears these words of mine and does not act on them will be like a foolish man who built his house on sand. The rain fell, and the floods came, and the winds blew and beat against that house, and it fell—and great was its fall!"

• **2 Timothy 3:14-17** (*Message*): Stick with what you learned and believed, sure of the integrity of your teachers—why, you took in the sacred Scriptures with your mother's milk! There's nothing like the written Word of God for showing you the way to salvation through faith in Christ Jesus. Every part of Scripture is God-breathed and useful one way or another—showing us truth, exposing our rebellion, correcting our mistakes, training us to live God's way. Through the Word we are put together and shaped up for the tasks God has for us.

• **Hebrews 4:12** (NRSV): Indeed, the word of God is living and active, sharper than any two-edged sword, piercing until it divides soul from spirit, joints from marrow; it is able to judge the thoughts and intentions of the heart.

• **James 1:22** (NRSV): But be doers of the word, and not merely hearers who deceive themselves.

Before You Teach This Lesson

What are your views on reading the Bible? How is it exciting? When is it tedious? What do you think is the best setting for reading Scripture?

Perhaps you heard Bible stories while growing up. These stories can become a part of the fabric of our faith and stick with us throughout our lives. As we mature, the Holy Spirit uses the texts that we learned as children to light our paths. Paul tells us that "all Scripture is inspired by God and is useful for teaching, for reproof, for correction, and for training in righteousness" (**2 Timothy 3:16**).

Think through these questions as you prepare to teach this session:

• Aside from when you are preparing a lesson or talk or writing something for church, how often do you read the Bible?

• What has the Holy Spirit revealed to you recently through Scripture?

• How has maturity changed how you view and interact with the Bible—mentally and spiritually?

• If you had only one hour to express to your students the importance of regular Scripture reading, what would you say?

Warm-up

Option 1: In or Out

<table>
<tr><td></td><td>What You'll Need
"In or Out" PowerPoint® game
(on the DVD)</td></tr>
</table>

Divide the youth into teams of four to five, and challenge the groups to decide whether each quotation in the game is from the Bible. Example: In or out: "I'm rubber; you're glue. Whatever you say bounces off of me and sticks to you."

1. In or out: "All men are created equal." (*Declaration of Independence*)

2. In or out: "My servant Isaiah has walked naked and barefoot for three years as a sign." (**Isaiah 20:3**)

3. In or out: "Cleanliness is next to godliness." (old proverb)

4. In or out: "Like a dog that returns to its vomit is a fool who reverts to his folly." (**Proverbs 26:11**)

5. In or out: "See what large letters I make." (**Galatians 6:11**)

6. In or out: "We must, indeed, all hang together, or most assuredly we shall all hang separately." (Benjamin Franklin)

7. In or out: "The driving is like that of Jehu son of Nimshi—he drives like a madman." (**2 Kings 9:20b,** NIV)

8. In or out: "Go away, baldhead! Go away, baldhead!" (**2 Kings 2:23**)

9. In or out: "God helps those who help themselves." (Benjamin Franklin)

Option 2: Human Knot

Divide youth into teams of six to twelve, keeping the teams roughly the same size. Have each group form a circle. Instruct the students to put their hands in the middle of their respective circle and grab the hands of two different people.

Once everyone is connected, challenge the teams to untangle themselves without letting go of the hands they are holding.

What You'll Need

"On Campus—The Bible" video from the DVD, DVD player or computer and projector

---

Video: On Campus—The Bible

Show the video "On Campus—The Bible" from the DVD; then have the youth get into groups of four to five to discuss these questions:

• Which of the students in this video do you most relate to? Why?

• Which of these students can you not relate to at all? Why?

• What reasons did the students give for reading or not reading the Bible? Which of these reasons make the most sense to you?

• If someone were to ask you why reading the Bible is important, how would you answer?

Teaching

Begin with prayer, thanking God for the gift of Scripture, and asking for the Lord's guidance as your youth read and learn about the Bible.

What You'll Need

"Glow: The Word" PowerPoint® show, copy of the Message Map (from the DVD) for everyone

Give this talk to the large group; or put it in your own words, using the key Scriptures and your own illustrations.

You may be familiar with the children's song that goes like this: "The B-I-B-L-E, yes that's the book for me; I stand alone on the Word of God, the B-I-B-L-E, Bible!" Today we're going to talk about it and why it's still the book for us.

Invite the youth to quickly form pairs or groups of three.

In your groups I want you to talk about your earliest memories of Bible stories. Maybe you were taught stories as a child that are still dear to you today. Maybe you have only recently become familiar with the stories in the Bible.

Give the youth a few minutes to discuss.

Here are some quick facts about the Bible. First off, the Bible isn't exactly a book—it's sixty-six individual books divided into two main sections: the Old Testament and New Testament. There are thirty-nine books in the Old Testament and twenty-seven in the New Testament. Jesus' birth is the event that separates the two testaments.

Write, "2 Timothy 3:14-17" on a large writing surface.

Look up **2 Timothy 3:14-17** in your Bible. If you do not have a Bible, find a neighbor who does.

The Bible isn't divided only into books but also into chapters. You'll notice that every Scripture reference is in three parts. The first is the book name—in this case, "2 Timothy."

The next is the chapter number, in this case "3." The colon divides the chapter number from the next part, which is the verse number, in this case "14–17."

*Invite a youth to read aloud **2 Timothy 3:14-17**.*

You may have noticed that the Scripture we just read is worded differently in the Bible you're holding. That's because many versions and translations of the Bible exist.

The books of the Bible were originally written in Hebrew or Greek. Translating these words and phrases from these languages into English can be done in several ways, so we have different translations. Some people prefer a straightforward translation such as the New Revised Standard Version or New International Version; some prefer the old-time language of the King James Version. And some prefer versions such as *The Message*, which phrase the text in contemporary language. What is important is having a translation that you understand. You should also find a Bible that has notes and study helps that make sense to you and give you a better understanding of what you're reading.

We're going to look at three ways the Bible is crucial to our lives and faith as Christians. The first is that the Bible is our source for **life information**. Have you ever put together a model car?* When you open the package, you see hundreds, even thousands of parts. Some of them are easy—it's obvious how these components go together with other parts. But most models include several parts that aren't so simple. The only way to know what to do with these parts is to read the instructions that come with the model.

You may use another illustration depending on your knowledge base and what interests your youth.

God uses the Bible to give us instructions on how to live. The Scripture we just read tells us that God's Word is "useful for teaching" and "training in righteousness." When we read the Bible, we learn about God's purpose for our lives and how God desires for us to live.

Divide youth into groups of three of four and have them discuss the questions about life information on their Message Maps.

Secondly, the promises that God makes in Scripture give us **life inspiration**. **Psalm 145:13** says, "The LORD is faithful in all [God's] words, and gracious in all [God's] deeds." In other words, the Lord keeps promises and reaches out to us in love. The Bible tells of God's promises to be present with us no matter what, to watch over us and deliver us from evil, and to give us eternal life in Jesus Christ. The Bible's story of grace and salvation inspires us to love, serve, and worship God and to live a life that pleases God.

Ask the youth to divide into different groups of three or four and to discuss the questions about life inspiration on their Message Map.

Inspiration isn't just about feeling good or optimistic. As Scripture inspires us to respond to God's love and grace, we are transformed. One reason that the Bible is the most popular book ever (or the most popular sixty-six books ever) and continues to be a best seller is because it has the power of **life transformation.** God's Holy Spirit works through the pages of Scripture to transform despair into hope, sadness into joy, and fear into courage.

Again, ask the youth to divide into different groups of three or four and to discuss the question about life transformation on their Message Map. Consider using this opportunity to tell a story from personal experience about how the Bible has changed your life or to invite someone from the congregation to tell such a story.

Before we wrap up, I want to read from **Psalm 119,** the Bible's longest chapter. **Psalm 119:9-11** says,

> How can young people keep their way pure?
>   By guarding it according to your word.
> With my whole heart I seek you;
>   do not let me stray from your commandments.
> I treasure your word in my heart,
>   so that I may not sin against you.

Let's pray.

> Gracious God, Thank you for the wonderful gift of your word. Teach us, inspire us, and transform us through your holy Scripture and help us make time each day to read and meditate on the Bible. Amen.

Unit 2: Room Raiders

"Room Raiders" is a five-session tour of the rooms in a typical house. Each room is a metaphor for some aspect of the Christian life. In addition to the PowerPoint® shows and teaching videos that go along with the sessions, the E|MERGE DVD also includes a Room Raiders "bumper," a short animation that you can use to introduce each session. For more about the five rooms you'll visit in this unit, read on.

The Family Room

This session encourages youth to look at what is special about their families and how they are in a unique position to improve their overall family vibe.

This session features the video "Amanda" (on the DVD).

The Kitchen

The kitchen is where people feed themselves physically. This session explores how we feed ourselves spiritually. Youth will look at all the ways they feed their souls.

The Bathroom

Much of what we do in the bathroom has to do with personal appearance. Youth will learn that God created them, loves them, and considers each of them beautiful.

This session features the video "Sarah" (on the DVD).

The Garage

A garage's contents can be valuable if they aren't junk. This session invites youth to think about the spiritual junk that clutters their lives.

The Bedroom

The bedroom is where we can shut the door and be alone. In this session, youth will learn the importance of integrity and what they do when no one is looking.

This session features the video "Choices" (on the DVD).

Room Raiders: The Family Room

The Big Idea

Many factors contribute to family stress, but youth are in a unique position to make their overall family vibe better.

Session Texts

- **Exodus 20:12** (NRSV): Honor your father and mother, so that your days may be long in the land that the Lord your God is giving you.

- **Luke 2:51** (NRSV): Then he went down with them and came to Nazareth, and was obedient to them. His mother treasured all these things in her heart.

- **Ephesians 6:1-3** (NRSV): Children, obey your parents in the Lord, for this is right. "Honor your father and mother"—this is the first commandment with a promise: "so that it may be well with you and that you may live long on the earth."

Before You Teach This Lesson

The family unit is the most basic structural element of our culture. Many adolescents' greatest strengths or shortcomings are tied directly or indirectly to family dynamics.

Reflect on the following questions as you prepare to teach this lesson:

- How would you describe your family from your growing-up years?

- What are your favorite memories of your family?

- Were you the oldest, youngest, middle, or only child? How did this trait influence your perspective on and relationship with your family?

- If you could have changed one thing about your family, what would it have been?

- If you had only one hour to convey biblical truth about family life to your students, what would you say and do?

Warm-up

Option 1: M&M® Challenge

Give each participant a bowl of M&Ms.

One at a time, have each youth put his or her hands in the socks so that one finger sticks out of each sock. Challenge each participant to eat as many M&Ms as possible by using just two fingers. Set a time limit, and see how many each person can eat in that time or time how long it takes each person to eat a certain number of M&Ms, such as twenty. To make the game more difficult, tell the players to use only their pinky fingers.

Option 2: Family Tree

Divide your group into teams, and let them work together to find the answers to the family connection questions on the slides.

Video: Amanda

Show the video "Amanda" from the DVD; then have the youth get into groups of four to five to discuss these questions:

• How is your family experience similar to Amanda's? How is it different? What makes Amanda's story extraordinary?

• What does Amanda's story tell you about what a family means?

• How is Amanda's faith an important part of her family story?

• What role does faith play in your family?

Teaching

Give this talk to the large group; or put it in your own words, using the key Scriptures and your own illustrations. Begin by updating the youth on what's going on in your youth ministry (PPT 3).

A "typical" or "traditional" family does not exist. No two families are alike, and families have various structures. Some of you live with your mom or your grandparents or your dad or your mom and dad. Some of you live with biological parents, while others of you might live with adoptive parents. You may also have stepparents. But many of you have had one or more male parental figures and one or more female parental figures; so when I use the terms *mom* and *dad,* understand that I'm referring to those parental figures in your life, even if they are not your biological or adoptive parents.

Even families with similar structures can be very different. The dynamics at work in a family that consists of a mother, a father, and two children can be vastly different from the dynamics at work in another two-parent, two-child household. *Normal* just isn't an adjective that we can use to describe families. One thing that all families do have in common is that they are not perfect. Every family could be better.

Look at your Message Map (PPT 4), and write in the boxes, according to the instructions, the thing you like most about your family and the thing you like the least. Keep these things in the back of your head as we continue.

Give the youth about twenty seconds to write.

The first point I want to make is that during this time in your life, things are changing. So many things happen to a person between sixth grade and graduation. You mature physically, mentally, and emotionally; your relationships with your parents change. Many of you are at an age when feeling abnormal is normal. Frankly, not one person has made it through the teenage years without feeling strange or out of place (PPT 5).

Message Map (on the DVD)
• Below the upward arrow, write the word *friends* (PPT 6).
• Below the downward arrow, write *parents* (PPT 7).

Here's what's happening: The influence that your friends and peers have on you is going up; the influence of your parents is decreasing. So your relationship with your parents is changing. Maybe you think that your dad's jokes—which used to be hilarious—are stupid; maybe your mom's once uncanny ability to heal any ailment now has its limitations. Your dad turns out not to be the superstar basketball player you once thought he was, and your mom ends up not knowing everything about everything. You used to hang out with your parents; you used to enjoy eating with them and going out with them. Family vacations used to be a blast—spending an entire week or more with your mom and dad and siblings. Your mom used to lay out clothes for you—now you're laying out clothes for her. You don't want to hang out with Dad because he wears sweatpants with dress shoes.

During times of change, people experience all kinds of emotions, including anger, sadness, and denial. Often change is accompanied by yelling and screaming. You may feel sad that things aren't the way they used to be—that some of the simple joys of childhood are now just memories. Your parents have probably experienced some sadness too because their little baby has grown up and they don't know where the time has gone. The transition from childhood to adulthood will probably involve some grieving for you and your parents.

But change isn't necessarily bad. Along with the grief come the joy and excitement of new challenges and opportunities. You and your parents will butt heads, but you'll be able to relate to your parents in new ways; you will come to better understand some of the struggles they face (PPT 8).

I want you to read aloud with me the verse that is on your Message Map, **Ephesians 6:1-3:** "Children, obey your parents in the Lord, for this is right. 'Honor your father and mother'—this is the first commandment with a promise: 'so that it may be well with you and you may live long on the earth.' "

I'd like you to circle a few key words in these verses. The first is *honor.* The Scripture says, "Honor your father and mother." The second word I want you to circle is *promise.* This passage reminds us that "Honor your father and mother" is the only one of the Ten Commandments that has a promise attached to it. It goes like this: If you honor your father and mother, things will go well and you will enjoy a long life. More specifically, if you honor your parents in the things you learn from them, you will be better off, because every rule has a benefit (PPT 9). For example, a mother tells her three-year-old, "Hold my hand. We're going to cross the street." What is the rule? "Hold my hand." What is the benefit? Not getting hit by a car.

Here's another example. Your father says that nothing good happens after eleven o'clock, so you have to be home by then. The rule is that you come home by eleven o'clock. The benefit is that you avoid the violent crime and accidents involving drunk drivers that happen more often late at night.

Another rule is: Don't have sex before marriage. The benefit is that you honor your body and your relationship with the person you might be having sex with, not to mention that you avoid sexually transmitted diseases and pregnancy out of wedlock.

No matter how much sense rules make, we can easily focus on how they limit us—how they keep us from enjoying ourselves and becoming adults. But rules are more about protection than setting limits. The trick is to understand that your parents truly have your best interests in mind when they make rules for you.

That thought brings me to my first point: **Listen to *their* hearts** (PPT 10). That is, listen to your parents' hearts when they tell you what to do and what not to do.

How many of your parents ask you stupid questions? How many of your parents make stupid rules? Here's the deal: When your mother or father gives you rules—no matter how stupid the rules seem—you need to listen to their heart and think about their intent. Ask yourself, *What are they really saying? What is behind this rule? Why are my parents telling me not to do this?* When you look at things from your parents' perspective, you may change how you feel about the rule. You still might not like it, but it may at least make sense to you.

Here is the second point: **Trust is earned** (PPT 11). I know that you've probably heard this saying before, but let's think about it. Most people judge a person's future actions based on what that person has done in the past. Your actions today will determine how people feel about you tomorrow. If you are lying today, people are not going to trust your word tomorrow. Pretty simple, right?

Think about it like this: I get a paycheck every other week, and I deposit that check into a checking account. Then I go pay my bills. I pay my house payment, my electric bill, my phone bill, and all the other bills that enable me to live comfortably in my house.

Now, let's say I have $16.76 left in my checking account after all my bills are paid. Then I go out to a big electronics store and see a new DVD that I want. The DVD costs $21, so I decide to write a check for it. What is going to happen to that check? It will bounce. Here's what happens when the check bounces: The bank charges a hefty fee, the store charges another big fee, and I still have to pay for the DVD because the money never came out of my account. When all is said and done, that $21 DVD could cost me close to $100!

Getting punished—however it happens at your house—is much the same as bouncing a check. You make a deposit into your "account" by doing things that are trustworthy. That means, when you say you are going somewhere with your friends and you go where you say you are going, you build trust with your parents. When your actions match your words, you put extra money into your "trust account."

When you are dishonest, you are writing a check that you can't cash. Not only are you punished for your dishonesty, but you also withdraw funds from your "trust account."

The account metaphor shows how to build trust in your account. When you get home late for the first time in a long time, your parents probably won't punish you severely. If you make regular deposits in your "trust account," you may never even have a curfew. Why set a curfew for someone who always returns home at a reasonable hour?

The third point is simple and is grounded in Christian truth: **Try honesty** (PPT 12). When I say, "Be honest," I mean that when you do something wrong at school, make sure that your parents find out before the principal calls. If you are falling behind in classes, let your parents know before the report card comes in the mail. If you wreck the car, come out with it. Don't try to hide the truth. Your parents will likely give you a lesser punishment if you are truthful from the beginning. More importantly, God expects honesty from each of us.

Number four is the **power of respect** (PPT 13). I wish we had more information on Jesus' early years. The Bible tells about his birth then pretty much skips right to Jesus at thirty, when he started his ministry. But Luke tells one story about Jesus as a twelve-year-old that gives us some clues about what Jesus may have been like as a teenager (PPT 14).

*Read aloud **Luke 2:51-52**.*

So what does this have to do with you? Well, it all comes back to respect. I believe that Jesus lived as a model of respect in his family. But many teens treat their parents disrespectfully.

Compare your interactions with friends and peers (even peers you don't like) to your interactions with your parents. Whom do you treat with more respect? Think about the perfect friend. You're thinking of someone who's loyal and trustworthy, right? Well, you'll probably never have friends who are more loyal, trustworthy, and supportive than your parents. Most adults you ask will say that they have had all kinds of friends come and go. Many of you will have boyfriends and girlfriends who exit your life as quickly as they entered it. But loving parents will stand by their children no matter what—even if their children run away from home or end up in jail.

You have the power to make your family situation better. You have more power than you probably know. Let's review:

- **Listen to *their* hearts** (PPT 10). When the rules your parents make seem unreasonable, take a moment and look at the situation from their perspective. You may better understand what is in your parents' hearts and see how their love is being expressed in the rule.

- **Trust is earned** (PPT 11). When you show your parents that you can be trusted, you will be given more trust in return.

- **Try honesty** (PPT 12). Misleading your parents never helps the family situation. Be up front, and take the stance of complete honesty.

- Finally, remember **the power of respect** (PPT 13). We model the life of Jesus when we respect our parents and submit to their authority (PPT 15).

Let's pray.

> Heavenly Father, thank you for our families and the people in our lives who love us. Help us to treat these people with love and respect, to be honest with them, and to listen to their hearts. Amen (PPT 16).

Room Raiders: The Kitchen

The Big Idea

The "You are what you eat" cliché is true. The kitchen is where we go to fill our bodies with the food that gives us energy. Likewise, in our spiritual lives, we need energy for daily living. We get this energy by developing habits that bring us closer to God.

Session Texts

• **Luke 6:47** (*Message*): "These words I speak to you are not mere additions to your life, homeowner improvements to your standard of living. They are foundation words, words to build a life on."

• **Hebrews 5:14** (NRSV): But solid food is for the mature, for those whose faculties have been trained by practice to distinguish good from evil.

• **James 1:4** (NRSV): Let endurance have its full effect, so that you may be mature and complete, lacking in nothing.

Before You Teach This Lesson

Good leadership begins with self-leadership. We cannot, with integrity, challenge students to spend time with God each day unless we ourselves practice spiritual disciplines.

Think through the following questions as you prepare to teach this lesson:

• How full is your spiritual gas tank? When (or how often) do you find yourself running on low?

• What spiritual disciplines do you practice regularly? How do these practices give you fuel for daily living?

• Why is this commitment to spiritual disciplines important to the teens you lead?

• If you only had one hour to talk to teenagers about daily spiritual habits, what would you want to convey?

Warm-up

What You'll Need
six crackers per participant, glasses of water

Option 1: Dry Whistle

Pick two to eight students to take part in this challenge. The goal is to eat and swallow all of the crackers and then be the first to whistle. The crackers will make their mouths dry, so whistling will be a challenge. Have plenty of water on hand so that contestants can clean their palettes.

Option 2: Ice-Cream Sifter

What You'll Need
one gallon or more of ice cream; several ice cream scoopers; several pairs of large pantyhose; one spoon and one cup or bowl for every participant

Beforehand, prepare one cup of ice cream in a bowl for every two participants.

Pair off the youth. Give each team a spoon and a prepared bowl. One player from each team will put one pair of nylon hose over his or her head and face his or her partner. The partner will feed the ice cream through the hose to the player wearing the hose. The first team to finish its bowl of ice cream wins. Afterward, hand out the rest of the spoons and bowls and let everyone enjoy some ice cream.

Teaching

Give this talk to the large group; or put it in your own words, using the key Scriptures and your own illustrations. Begin by updating the youth on what's going on in your youth ministry (PPT 3).

This is the second session in our series called "Room Raiders" (PPT 1). In this series, we are going into the different rooms of our house. Last time, we visited the family room and discussed relationships with parents. We talked about how the influence your parents have over you is going down while the influence that your friends have over you is going up. As this change happens, friction and even some grieving can happen between parents and children.

Later in this series, we'll visit the bathroom, garage, and bedroom. But tonight we're in the kitchen. We're looking at the stuff we eat and take into our bodies—physically and, more importantly, spiritually.

What do you do in the kitchen? You eat snacks and fix meals. For many of us, eating is a matter of habit. We eat at the same times each day, we have our favorite snacks several times a week, and many of us have the same drink with our meal every night. A lot of families have certain meals that they prepare every week. And our kitchen habits aren't limited to what we eat. The jobs that different members of the family do to prepare a meal and clean up afterward can also become daily habits. How many of you are responsible for setting the table or doing the dishes?

All of these habits are important parts of how we feed ourselves so that we can grow and stay healthy.

Message Map (on the DVD)

Your Message Map lists various ways we must grow and stay healthy. Think about each of these areas of your life. How do you feed yourself physically, mentally, socially, and emotionally?

Feeding ourselves spiritually is similar to feeding ourselves in other ways—it involves daily habits and practices. What and how much you eat directly affect your physical health (and, to some extent, your mental health). Eating around the table with your family and working together to prepare and clean up after meals strengthen your social and emotional health. Likewise, by feeding yourself spiritually, making spiritual practices daily habits, you strengthen your spiritual health and your relationship with God.

Many of you already feed yourselves spiritually: You come to church once a week, you participate in worship, and you say prayers. These practices become habits when we give them over to God. Maybe you come to church only because your friends are here or because it's part of your weekend routine. But if you surrender your church-going to God, you'll find yourself drawn to worship, looking forward to worship.

If we don't stop to spend time with God and to practice spiritual disciplines, we will be overwhelmed by conflict, busyness, and stress. But if you make time to hang out with God and develop spiritual habits, you'll have peace and satisfaction. You will receive God's insight, and your faith will replace your worry.

Time with God truly changes your life (PPT 4). You shouldn't develop spiritual habits out of a sense of obligation or because it's what you should do as a Christian. You should hang out with God because the Father loves you and wants to spend time with you. Spiritual habits are how we respond to God's love and grace.

You also need to know that developing these habits is a lifelong task. Let's step out of the kitchen for a while and think of our relationship with God as a road trip. A lot of college students like road trips. They hop in whoever's car has the best chance of getting back home and take off. Sometimes they have a destination, such as a concert or basketball game, then turn around and come home; sometimes they don't have one. But no matter where they go, friends who take road trips together learn more about one another and grow closer. They become more open about what's going on in their lives and become more trusting of one another.

Maybe we should think of our relationship with God as a road trip. We shouldn't worry too much about our destination or what we're getting out of the relationship. We should focus on the journey itself and enjoy the time we spend alone with God. We should listen to God and learn about the Lord. We should also open up and talk to God about our lives—our joys and struggles and questions.

For sure, participating in a Christian community is important to growing in your faith; but the community cannot just drag you along. You must accept some responsibility for your spiritual growth.

For example, let's say that I told you I made some mean macaroni and cheese (PPT 5). So every week, you come to my house to eat my mac and cheese. You like it so much that you want to suck it up with a straw and lick the bowl.

All of a sudden, you're eating mac and cheese almost every day. You get to the point when if you can't have my mac and cheese, your stomach rumbles. With every meal that isn't my macaroni and cheese, you get frustrated. You can't concentrate in class. You get grumpy and bite people's heads off when they talk to you.

After a while, we get together again, you eat some of my mac and cheese, and you get your fix. But the satisfaction doesn't last. Before long, you're getting cranky and your stomach's rumbling again. And what happens if you move to another city or go off to college or join the military and I'm not there to make mac and cheese for you?

My goal is to teach you how to make macaroni and cheese yourself. It's important that you develop spiritual habits that you can take with you when you leave this congregation. While participating in a faith community is an important part of being a Christian, that identity is about much more than going to church—it is a way of life. We all need ways to remain nourished spiritually even when we're alone.

The best way to develop spiritual habits—to get into the kitchen every day to make mac and cheese—is to **make spending time each day with God a priority** (PPT 6).

How many of you make it a priority to get dressed in the morning? How important are showering and brushing your teeth to you? How important is eating three meals a day? How crucial is watching your favorite television show each week?

The things we make time for tell us a lot about what we value. If we truly value our relationship with God, we need to make time with God a priority.

Let's look to Scripture (PPT 7).

*Read aloud or ask a youth to read aloud **Hebrews 5:14.***

Hebrews tells us that as we mature in faith, we must also mature in how we feed our souls. If we want to grow as Christians, we can't just expect other people to spoon-feed us. We can't just show up at worship once a week and go through the motions. We need something more substantial; we need to establish habits and disciplines that connect us with God and with other Christians and that help us grow in faith. The solid food that the writer of Hebrews is talking about includes practices of prayer and devotion and participation in a church community (PPT 8).

Let's review. Just as our bodies need food, so do our souls. We feed our souls by spending time with God through prayer, Scripture reading, worship, and other practices of the faith. These spiritual disciplines are the "solid food" that enables us to grow in faith.

Let's pray.

> God, we need more of you in our lives. We need to bask in your presence, allow you into our hearts and minds, and give our lives over to you. Help us this week to spend time with you each day and to let you transform our lives. Amen.

Room Raiders: The Bathroom

The Big Idea

Image is everything in our culture. Both guys and girls spend hours in the bathroom, crafting the image that they will present to the world. At times, the beautiful person whom God has created is lost under layers of masks. Youth need to be reminded that God loves the person beneath the masks and knows each of us intimately and personally.

Session Texts

• **Genesis 3:6-11** (*Message*): When the Woman saw that the tree looked like good eating and realized what she would get out of it—she'd know everything!—she took and ate the fruit and then gave some to her husband, and he ate.

Immediately the two of them did "see what's really going on"—saw themselves naked! They sewed fig leaves together as makeshift clothes for themselves.

When they heard the sound of God strolling in the garden in the evening breeze, the Man and his Wife hid in the trees of the garden, hid from God.

God called to the Man: "Where are you?"

He said, "I heard you in the garden and I was afraid because I was naked. And I hid."

God said, "Who told you you were naked? Did you eat from that tree I told you not to eat from?"

• **1 Samuel 16:7b** (NRSV): The LORD does not see as mortals see; they look on the outward appearance, but the LORD looks on the heart.

• **Luke 6:47** (*Message*): "These words I speak to you are not mere additions to your life, homeowner improvements to your standard of living. They are foundation words, words to build a life on."

• **Romans 5:8** (NRSV): God proves [God's] love for us in that while we still were sinners Christ died for us.

Before You Teach This Lesson

Reflect on these questions:

- Think back to when you were in middle school or high school. How important was your image to you?

- What "looks" did you go for when you were a teenager? What images or personas did you try to present to others?

- Right now, how important is the image you project to others? What perspective have you gained since your teenage years?

- If you had only one hour to talk to your students about self-image, what are the most important points you'd want to convey?

Warm-up

Option 1: Toilet Tag

What You'll Need
a large space

Define the boundaries of your playing area; then select someone to be "it." As in a normal game of tag, "it" attempts to tag another player, making that player "it." In this game, a person cannot be tagged if he or she squats (as if sitting on a toilet). However, a player can stay in the squat position for only five seconds at a time.

Option 2: Extreme Makeover

What You'll Need
variety of makeup (such as lipstick, blush, and eyeshadow), hair gel, trash bags, towels and facial tissues for clean-up

Beforehand, try to find a makeup salesperson who may be able to give you plenty of makeup samples to make this game work.

Divide the youth into guy-girl pairs. (If the girls outnumber the guys, create teams with one boy and more than one girl; if the guys outnumber girls, put some girls in charge of making over more than one boy.)

The purpose of this game is for the girls to give the boys a new look with makeup and hair gel. Allow the girls three or four minutes to work on the guys; then judge the winner by show of applause.

Teaching

What You'll Need

The video "Sarah" from the DVD, DVD player or computer and projector

Give this talk to the large group; or paraphrase it, using the key Scriptures and your own illustrations. Start by updating the youth on what's going on in your youth ministry (PPT 3).

One of the key texts throughout this Room Raiders series has been **Luke 6:47** (PPT 4): "These words I speak to you are not mere additions to your life, homeowner improvements to your standard of living. They are foundation words, words to build a life on" (*Message*).

So we aren't just visiting these rooms to clean up or decorate. We're getting down to the bare studs and making sure that the foundation is secure. This time, we're going to look at the bathroom (PPT 2).

Message Map (on the DVD)

Close your eyes, and picture your house or apartment. Picture yourself walking through the house to your favorite toilet lid. Put the lid down, take a seat on the throne, and take a look around the room. Look at the shower, the mirror, and the sink; and think about what you spend most of your time doing. Do you primp? Do you style your hair? Do you get in and out as quickly as possible? Do you use a hair dryer, makeup, or curling iron?

Allow time for the students to answers on their Message Maps.

Think about who and what you see when you look in the mirror while you're getting ready each day. What is the number-one thing that you wish you could change about your appearance?

Allow time for the students to answer on their Message Maps. Then, depending on the comfort level of your group, invite the youth to reveal to a person sitting next to them what they would like to change; or invite volunteers to tell the group what they wish to change about themselves.

Dropping by the bathroom gives us a great opportunity to talk about self-image. The most important thing I can tell you about it is that you have been created in God's image. What does that truth mean? Does it mean that you have God's cheekbones or hair color? Not exactly.

Think about your parents. Which of you would say that you look more like your mom? Which of you would say that you look more like your dad? Let's say you look like your mom. Does that trait mean that your dad's image isn't a part of your genetic makeup? No. You have characteristics of both of your parents, regardless of how much you look like either one of them.

You also have characteristics of God. As human beings, God has given us gifts such as creativity and compassion and reasoning. We can be assured that God crafted us, loves us, and sees beauty in each of us.

But sometimes we have a hard time remembering that God loves us and considers us beautiful. When we have a negative self-image, we often project our negative feelings about ourselves onto God and assume that God feels the same way.

Brennan Manning, in *Posers, Fakers, & Wannabes* says:

> If we feel hatred for ourselves, it only makes sense that God hates us. Right?
>
> No, not so much.
>
> It's no good assuming God feels about us the way we feel about ourselves—unless we love ourselves intensely and freely with complete wisdom and never-ending compassion.

We need to understand that just because we don't feel good about ourselves—just because we would like to change something—that God doesn't feel that way about us. God loves you "intensely and freely, with complete wisdom and never-ending compassion."

Another important thing to remember is that God doesn't make junk. Thus you are not junk. No matter how you feel about yourself, no matter what you see when you look in the mirror, you are God's beloved creation and God loves you with an intense love.

People have always struggled with body image. Think about Adam and Eve in the Garden of Eden. What was the first thing they did after they sinned in the garden? They recognized that they were naked and covered themselves up. They were ashamed. Unfortunately, shame is too often associated with our bodies (PPT 5). Let's look at **Genesis 3:6-11** from *The Message:*

> When the Woman saw that the tree looked like good eating and realized what she would get out of it—she'd know everything!—she took and ate the fruit and then gave some to her husband, and he ate.

> Immediately the two of them did "see what's really going on"—saw themselves naked! They sewed fig leaves together as makeshift clothes for themselves (PPT 6).

> When they heard the sound of God strolling in the garden in the evening breeze, the Man and his Wife hid in the trees of the garden, hid from God.

> God called to the Man: "Where are you?"

> He said, "I heard you in the garden and I was afraid because I was naked. And I hid."

> God said, "Who told you you were naked? Did you eat from that tree I told you not to eat from?"

At least no other people were around when Adam and Eve discovered that they were naked. Being surrounded by friends and peers who are developing in different ways and at different rates makes body-image issues even more complicated. Many of us find ourselves wondering, *Am I normal? Is my body normal?*

The answer to that question is "No, you're not normal." I say so because there is no such thing as normal. There is no normal way to develop emotionally, physically, or spiritually.

You also need to know that God has been pursuing you since before you were born. God is actively chasing you. God wants to be in a relationship with you. God likes you. And when you let God catch you—when you accept Christ's saving grace and commit to living in relationship with God—you become a new creation. The old passes away and you are made new.

Video: "Sarah"

Show the video "Sarah" from the DVD; then have the youth get into groups of four to five, in which each group consists of all boys or all girls, to discuss these questions:

• How can you relate to Sarah and her experience as a teen?

• Sarah's self-image was tarnished when her father told her she had "fat knees." How do your friends and family affect how you feel about your body, either positively or negatively?

• Sarah realizes that the media's portrayal of the ideal body had an affect on her body image. How are the perfect bodies that we see on television shows and magazines unrealistic?

• Sarah was ultimately transformed through her relationship with God. What does being created by the Lord in God's image mean to you?

When the discussion winds down, continue with the teaching.

To get a better sense of just how much God loves us, let's look at **Romans 5:8** (PPT 7), which says, "God proves [God's] love for us in that while we still were sinners Christ died for us."

You are worth dying for. Jesus made the ultimate sacrifice for you. Christ's love will not change no matter the color of your skin, where you were born, who your parents are, how many zits are on your face, how straight your teeth are, whether you wear glasses, or whether you wear expensive clothes (PPT 8).

According to **1 Samuel 16:7,** "The Lord does not see as mortals see; they look on the outward appearance, but the Lord looks on the heart."

Look me in the eyes. There is not one ugly person in this room. I'm dead serious. All of you are beautiful, and none of you is disposable. God loves you no matter what. You are not cheap; you were bought with a price.

You are made in God's image—you and everyone else in this room. You should not treat any of your brothers and sisters in Christ as anything less than people made in God's image.

Let's pray.

> God, we thank you for the beautiful diversity in this room
> and for all of the ways you have made us unique. You do not
> make junk, but we sometimes forget how much you love us
> and value us. Help us always to remember that we are
> created in your image, that you pursue us, and that we are
> new creations worth dying for. We thank you and love you.
> Amen.

Room Raiders: The Garage

The Big Idea

Challenge your youth to take an honest look at the junk that tends to pile up in their lives, so that they may dispose of the sin that gets in the way of what God desires for them.

Session Texts

- **Deuteronomy 6:5** (*Message*): Love God, your God, with your whole heart: love [the Lord] with all that's in you, love [God] with all you've got!

- **Ezekiel 11:19** (NRSV): I will give them one heart, and put a new spirit within them; I will remove the heart of stone from their flesh and give them a heart of flesh.

- **Matthew 7:16-17** (NRSV): You will know them by their fruits. Are grapes gathered from thorns, or figs from thistles? In the same way, every good tree bears good fruit, but the bad tree bears bad fruit.

- **Luke 6:47** (*Message*): "These words I speak to you are not mere additions to your life, homeowner improvements to your standard of living. They are foundation words, words to build a life on."

- **Ephesians 4:26-27** (*Message*): Go ahead and be angry. You do well to be angry—but don't use your anger as fuel for revenge. And don't stay angry. Don't go to bed angry. Don't give the Devil that kind of foothold in your life.

Before You Teach This Lesson

We all have that place in our home where we store junk. It may be your attic, a closet, the top drawer of your dresser, or your garage.

Think through these questions as you prepare to teach this lesson:

- Whom in your life do you need to forgive? Do you hold grudges that keep you from growing in your relationship with Christ? What do you need to do to find peace in that relationship?

- How do you deal with your anger? Do you have any unresolved anger? How could you deal with this anger?

• How disciplined is your spiritual life? Are you able to find time each day or week to spend time with God?

Warm-up

Option 1: Boxed Up

What You'll Need
three to five cardboard boxes per team, one roll of packing tape per team, durable scissors

Instruct the youth to pair off. Each pair should decide who will be the packer and who will be boxed up. Give each pair three to five cardboard boxes and a roll of packing tape. Explain that the goal is to see who can most neatly and durably box up his or her teammate. Allow three or four minutes for packing. Determine the winner by show of applause. After the game, use scissors to carefully unpack the boxed-up players.

Option 2: Bunched Up

What You'll Need
music and a CD or MP3 player

While the music plays, the students should walk around the room, mingling. Each time the music stops, clap a different number of times of times. The students should then get into groups based on the number of claps. (For example, if you clap five times, the teens should get into groups of five.) Eliminate from the game the youth who are unable to fit into a group. End the game when only two persons remain; declare these youth the winners.

Teaching

Give this talk to the large group; or put it in your own words, using the key Scriptures and your own illustrations. Begin by updating the youth on what's going on in your youth ministry (PPT 3).

Option: Writing or painting the main points on the face of large moving boxes may help you communicate this message more effectively. When you introduce a new point, bring out the appropriate box and stack it so that the words face the students.

Let's pray.

God, thank you for the opportunity to meet together, talk about you, and learn from you today. Help us to experience your presence in new ways as you open our hearts and minds. We give you all the praise. Amen.

For this session, you'll need your Bibles. We'll be jumping around a lot. If you start to get lost, raise your hand or refer to your Message Map.

So far, in this Room Raiders series we've visited the family room (PPT 4), the kitchen (PPT 5), an the bathroom (PPT 6). Today, we'll be in the garage (PPT 7). Next time, we'll be in the bedroom.

Turn to **Luke 6:47:** "These words I speak to you are not mere additions to your life, homeowner improvements on your standard of living. They are foundation words, words to build a life on" (*Message*).

In a lot of households, the garage is where people let their junk pile up. Other households have an attic or closet that serves the same purpose. At your age, you might not think of the garage as your own. Maybe your family's garage or attic is so cluttered that your parents won't let you go out there. But chances are that you have some space where junk can accumulate. Maybe it's a junk drawer, a closet, or just a designated space in your room. Maybe you could describe your entire room as a junk space. Today we're going to talk about these cluttered storage spaces—the garages of our lives. We're going to talk about how stuff seems to pile up and how we need to clean out the junk from time to time. If we don't, it will overtake our lives.

Let's take a look at **Deuteronomy 6:5:** "You shall love the Lord your God with all your heart, and with all your soul, and with all your might" (PPT 8). *The Message,* a popular paraphrase of the Bible translates this verse as, "Love God, your God, with your whole heart: love [God] with all that's in you, love [God] with all you've got!"

Your "whole heart" is like your garage. It's where you store your deepest thoughts and feelings. What you store in your heart comes out in your character (PPT 9). Jesus says in **Matthew 7:16-17** that good trees bear good fruit and bad trees bear bad fruit. That idea sounds simple enough, but it's an important point. What we keep in our hearts determines our attitudes and behaviors. If we take care of our hearts, we will have healthier relationships with God and others and our faith will be apparent to everyone we meet. If we don't tend our hearts, our relationships will suffer and we will be more vulnerable to temptation and despair.

Let's get rid of this junk we keep in our hearts. The first type of junk that we need to clean out is being unforgiving or holding **grudges** (PPT 10). We've all been in situations where we've had to forgive someone, and we've all been in situations when we've had to ask for forgiveness. When someone, particularly someone close to us, hurts us, we are often tempted not to forgive. Maybe we think that by not forgiving, we will hurt the person who has hurt us. But we just end up hurting ourselves. Take a moment to think about anyone whom you haven't forgiven. What did these persons do? You may have every right to be angry, and forgiving these persons may be difficult. But when you do allow yourself to forgive them, you will let go of a heavy burden and will be able to truly begin healing (PPT 11).

Ephesians 4:26-27, as it is paraphrased in *The Message,* reads, "Go ahead and be angry. You do well to be angry—but don't use your anger as fuel for revenge. And don't stay angry. Don't go to bed angry. Don't give the Devil that kind of foothold in your life."

Take a moment to write on your Message Map in response to the questions about grudges.

Give the youth a few minutes to answer the questions on their Message Maps; then have them discuss their answers in pairs or groups of three.

The second box of junk that we need to get rid of is **sloppiness** (PPT 12). Be honest: How many of you have a difficult time with self-discipline? Many of us are good at starting things but have a hard time sticking to them, whether in learning to play an instrument, taking part in a sports team, or doing a home-improvement project. The same is true of spiritual practice. We grow in our relationship with God through holy habits such as daily prayer and Scripture reading. These habits require discipline. If we want to be disciplined, we need to rid ourselves of laziness and any distractions that keep us from being focused on our relationship with God.

Take a moment to write on your Message Map in response to the questions about sloppiness.

Give the youth a few minutes to answer the questions on their Message Maps; then have them discuss their answers in pairs or groups of three.

Being unforgiving and being undisciplined are only two types of junk that clutter our hearts; we could talk about many more if we had time. We need to look inside, to look at all the junk that we've let pile up. Then we need to clean out the garage (PPT 13). We need to get rid of all the junk that gets in the way of our relationship with God.

Let's pray.

> God, we know that you desire for us to live a full and abundant life. We thank you for the gift of your Holy Spirit, who lives in our hearts. Help us to clean out the junk so that we can give ourselves fully to you. Amen.

Room Raiders: The Bedroom

The Big Idea

Integrity involves not only acting in a way that's consistent with your words and beliefs but also acting that way when no one is looking. Maintaining our integrity is an important part of our identity as Christians.

Session Texts

• **Joshua 7:1, 4-7, 10-11, 19-21** (NRSV): The Israelites broke faith in regard to the devoted things: Achan son of Carmi son of Zabdi son of Zerah, of the tribe of Judah, took some of the devoted things; and the anger of the LORD burned against the Israelites. . . .

So about three thousand of the people went up there; and they fled before the men of Ai. The men of Ai killed about thirty-six of them, chasing them from outside the gate as far as Shebarim and killing them on the slope. The hearts of the people melted and turned to water.

Then Joshua tore his clothes, and fell to the ground on his face before the ark of the LORD until the evening, he and the elders of Israel; and they put dust on their heads. Joshua said, "Ah, Lord GOD! Why have you brought this people across the Jordan at all, to hand us over to the Amorites so as to destroy us? Would that we had been content to settle beyond the Jordan!" . . .

The LORD said to Joshua, "Stand up! Why have you fallen upon your face? Israel has sinned; they have transgressed my covenant that I imposed on them. They have taken some of the devoted things; they have stolen, they have acted deceitfully, and they have put them among their own belongings." . . .

Then Joshua said to Achan, "My son, give glory to the LORD God of Israel and make confession to [God]. Tell me now what you have done; do not hide it from me." And Achan answered Joshua, "It is true; I am the one who sinned against the LORD God of Israel. This is what I did: when I saw among the spoil a beautiful mantle from Shinar, and two hundred shekels of silver, and a bar of gold weighing fifty shekels, then I coveted them and took them. They now lie hidden in the ground inside my tent, with the silver underneath."

- **Proverbs 11:3** (*Message*): The integrity of the honest keeps them on track; the deviousness of crooks brings them to ruin.

- **Acts 5:1-6** (NRSV): But a man named Ananias, with the consent of his wife Sapphira, sold a piece of property; with his wife's knowledge, he kept back some of the proceeds, and brought only a part and laid it at the apostles' feet. "Ananias," Peter asked, "why has Satan filled your heart to lie to the Holy Spirit and to keep back part of the proceeds of the land? While it remained unsold, did it not remain your own? And after it was sold, were not the proceeds at your disposal? How is it that you have contrived this deed in your heart? You did not lie to us but to God!" Now when Ananias heard these words, he fell down and died. And great fear seized all who heard of it. The young men came and wrapped up his body, then carried him out and buried him.

- **Romans 6:23** (NRSV): For the wages of sin is death, but the free gift of God is eternal life in Christ Jesus our Lord.

Before You Teach This Lesson

Youth are great judges of integrity. For some reason, teenagers can sniff out fakers like police dogs sniff out narcotics. If our actions are inconsistent with our words and beliefs, our youth will catch us and call us out. We need to set an example for the students we work with by maintaining our integrity even when doing so is difficult or uncomfortable. Jesus said that "a student is not above his teacher, but everyone who is fully trained will be like his teacher" (**Luke 6:40, NIV**). These words both encourage and haunt teachers, mentors, and student ministers.

Think through these questions as you prepare to teach this lesson:

- When you think of people of integrity, who comes to mind? What do you admire most about these people?

- When, if ever, have you been tempted to mislead or hide something from your youth? How did you deal with these temptations?

- What can you do to make your actions more consistent with what you say and believe?

• If you had only one hour to teach students the importance of integrity, what would you say?

Warm-up

Option 1: Room Raider

What You'll Need
pictures of students' bedrooms taken by the students

Beforehand, contact your youth and ask them to take a few pictures of their bedroom. They can e-mail the pictures to you or bring in prints. Tell them that they should not clean their rooms before snapping the photo, but try to capture what their bedroom looks like on an average day. When the youth arrive, scatter the pictures on a table or the floor, and have the students guess which of their peers each picture belongs to. Give the youth a few minutes to match the photos; then ask the students who provided the pictures to say which were theirs.

Option 2: Dream Bedroom

What You'll Need
paper, pens or pencils, and colored pencils or markers

Divide your youth into groups of four to five, and challenge each group to design the ideal bedroom. Explain that money is no object and that the only condition is that they must select a theme. The teams may create a chart or blueprint, do a perspective drawing, write a description, or do any combination of these things. Give the teams about five minutes to work; then allow each team to present its idea. Affirm each group's creativity, and ask the teams to explain why they chose certain features.

Video: Choices

What You'll Need
The video "Choices" from the DVD, DVD player or computer and projector

Show the video "Choices" from the DVD; then have the youth divide into groups of four to five to discuss these questions:

• Which of the students interviewed in this video do you relate to the most? Why?

- Which of these students can you not relate to at all? Why?

- When have you done something that you knew was wrong?

- One student, talking about a time when he did something he knew was wrong, says that even though he didn't get caught, he didn't feel right about what he did. How do you feel after you do something that you know is wrong? Does how you feel depend on whether you get caught?

Teaching

Give this talk to the large group; or put it in your own words, using the key Scriptures and your own illustrations. Begin by updating the youth on what's going on in your youth ministry (PPT 3).

We are now at the end of the Room Raiders series. We've had a great time running through the rooms in a typical house: the family room (PPT 4), the kitchen (PPT 5), the bathroom (PPT 6), and the garage (PPT 7). Today, we'll be making our final stop in the bedroom (PPT 8).

Take a moment to describe your teenage bedroom. What did it look like? What did you love about your bedroom? What didn't you like? What made that space special?

Raise your hand if the following is true for you:

- You share a bedroom with a sibling.

- You get to have a room to yourself.

- You got to paint and decorate your room.

- You had no say about the paint (or wallpaper), carpet (or other flooring), or furniture in your room.

- The basic look of your room has not changed since preschool.

- Your room is almost all the time clean.

- Your room is sometimes clean; you straighten up every few weeks.

- Your room is never clean.

• Cleaning your room involves shoving everything in your closet.

• You made your bed this morning.

Let me ask one more question: How many of you have some sort of "space" on the Internet, such as a MySpace or Xanga page or a blog or other personal website?

Allow the youth to answer by raising their hands.

One reason these online communities have become so popular is that they give you (and anyone else in the world) an opportunity to own space on the Internet. It's space that is completely yours and can be modified, decorated, or designed any way you like. Most of us hunger in some way for space that is uniquely ours and that we can control and modify.

Today, in the bedroom—in our personal space— we're talking about integrity (PPT 9). On your Message Map, you'll notice a simple definition of integrity that we'll be using during this talk: **Integrity is who you are when no one is looking.**

We're going to look at the Old Testament story of Achan, found in the Book of Joshua. The Israelites were celebrating a great victory in the battle of Jericho (when the "walls came tumblin' down"), but with God's blessings came conditions. God told the Israelites that they were to keep none of the treasure in the city of Jericho and that all of the precious metals were to be devoted to God.

Achan was an Israelite and was well aware of God's rule. Still he couldn't resist temptation and stole some gold for himself. Achan returned to his tent, which was essentially his bedroom, and buried the gold. He stole from God when no one was looking.

The Israelites advanced from Jericho to the next city, Ai. They were confident going into battle against Ai, which was a smaller and weaker city than Jericho. In fact, Joshua, the leader of the Israelites, sent only a few thousand troops into battle. But it didn't go as planned. The army from Ai quickly routed the Israelite troops and sent them fleeing. Any confidence the Israelites had gained after the battle of Jericho had faded.

What went wrong? In **Joshua 7:10-11,** God explains to Joshua why the Israelites were defeated so badly.

*Read aloud or ask a youth to read aloud **Joshua 7:10-11** (PPT 10–15).*

God punished Israel because Achan disobeyed God's command by stealing and hiding gold from Jericho. But Achan didn't get away with his crimes. God singled Achan out, Achan confessed, and God ordered the Israelites to execute him by stoning him and burning him. As you can see, God takes integrity very seriously.

A similar story is found in the Book of Acts in the New Testament.

*Read aloud **Acts 4:32-34** (the believers' agreement to share their possessions). Then ask a youth to read aloud **Acts 5:1-6** (PPT 16–18).*

Ananias and Sapphira were punished not because they kept some of their money but because they lied about it. They made a commitment to God to give all of their possessions to the church, but they didn't honor their commitment. When no one was looking, they sold some property and kept the money. Like Achan, they didn't get away with it. Even if they had been able to hide their actions from the leaders of the early church, they would still have been accountable to God.

The Lord will probably not strike us dead for breaking a promise or failing to live up to a commitment, but these Scriptures nonetheless teach us important lessons about integrity. One lesson we can learn from these stories is that **our integrity is often tested at the high points and low points in our lives** (PPT 19). Achan was first tested when times were good. Israel had just won a great battle and felt the full presence and blessing of God. But when times are good, we often feel invincible—like we can get away with anything—and we are susceptible to temptation. After the fall of Jericho, gold was plentiful and easy to come by. Achan saw an opportunity to steal some gold, and he took it.

Achan was tested again when times were bad. Israel lost what should have been an easy battle and was uncertain about its relationship with God. Achan could have admitted his crime, but doing so would have required courage and a willingness to accept punishment. Instead, Joshua had to force a confession from Achan.

The second lesson is that **our integrity affects others** (PPT 20). What we do when no one is looking can have an effect on our friends, our families, and our communities. In Achan's case, his lack of integrity affected God's relationship with the entire nation of Israel. In the case of Ananias and Sapphira, the money they secretly withheld could have been used to further the mission of the church. When we are dishonest about things we have said and done and when our actions don't match our words and beliefs, we betray the people who know us and depend on us.

Finally: **A lack of integrity brings death** (PPT 21). Again, the congregation won't stone you if they find out you've stolen something; and God won't necessarily strike you dead if you are dishonest. But Paul, in his letter to the church in Rome, makes an important point.

Read aloud or ask a youth to read aloud **Romans 6:23** *(PPT 22).*

In other words, the result of sin is death. Sin may not kill us physically, but it can kill relationships, credibility, trust, and other important aspects of life. Fortunately, Paul also says that the gift of God is eternal life and that this gift is available to each of us.

To close, let's look at one more Scripture that deals with the importance of integrity.

Read aloud or ask a youth to read aloud **Proverbs 11:3** *from* The Message *(PPT 23).*

I'd like you to memorize this verse and apply it to your lives this week. Integrity brings us closer to God and improves our relationship with others; when we lack integrity, we allow sin and death to take over our lives.

Let's pray.

> God, we know that you are a God of integrity. Help us to live lives of integrity this week through our words and actions. Guard our hearts, and keep them safe from any hint of sin. Amen.

Unit 3: The Call

"The Call" is a five-session study of how God calls us and how we should respond. In addition to the PowerPoint® shows and teaching videos that go along with the sessions, the EMERGE DVD also includes a "bumper," a short animation that you can use to introduce each session. The sessions in this unit include "Knowing God," "You Are Here," "Can You Hear Me Now?" "Keeping the Lines Clear," and "Called to Follow."

Knowing God

A difference exists between knowing God and knowing about God. If we truly want to know the Lord, we must orient our hearts and minds toward God.

You Are Here

The Christian life is a journey, and God calls us to advance along our journey of faith. To answer God's call, we must first identify where we are so that we can figure out where we need to go.

Can You Hear Me Now?

Sometimes we struggle to hear what the Lord is telling us and wonder whether God is listening to what we are saying. But God is always present with us and always listening to us, even when the Lord seems distant. Through worship, we become better aware of God's presence.

Keeping the Lines Clear

The realm of communication has four major players: the sender, the receiver, the message, and the noise. In our conversations with God, we need to eliminate the noise so that we can accurately and consistently hear God's voice.

Called to Follow

Christ calls us to follow him; so our lives are not our own. Rather, Jesus has commissioned us to a life of service to God's kingdom.

This session features the video "Emma" (on the DVD).

The Call: Knowing God

The Big Idea

God wants to know us and be known by us. Knowing the Lord is not simply a matter of doing, saying, or professing the right things; rather it involves orienting our minds and hearts toward God.

Session Texts

- **Psalm 46:10** (NRSV): "Be still, and know that I am God!
    I am exalted among the nations,
    I am exalted in the earth."

- **Jeremiah 31:33-34** (*Message*): "This is the brand-new covenant that I will make with Israel when the time comes. I will put my law within them—write it on their hearts!—and be their God. And they will be my people. They will no longer go around setting up schools to teach each other about God. They'll know me firsthand, the dull and the bright, the smart and the slow. I'll wipe the slate clean for each of them. I'll forget they ever sinned!" God's Decree.

- **Matthew 7:21-23** (NRSV): "Not everyone who says to me, 'Lord, Lord,' will enter the kingdom of heaven, but only the one who does the will of my Father in heaven. On that day, many will say to me, 'Lord, Lord, did we not prophesy in your name, and cast out demons in your name, and do many deeds of power in your name?' Then I will declare to them, 'I never knew you; go away from me, you evildoers.' "

Before You Teach This Lesson

How would you describe your relationship with God? How well do you and God know each other?

All of our acts of mercy, worship, devotion, and justice are important to our spiritual maturity; but just because we pray every morning, go to church each week, and make a habit of volunteering our time to serve others doesn't mean that we know God. To truly know the Lord, we must pray, worship, and serve with our hearts and minds set on God.

e|Merge 1.0: Director's Guide

Think through these questions as you prepare to teach this session:

- How do you set your mind and heart on God when you pray or participate in worship?

- How is your experience of worship different when you focus on God than when you just go through the motions?

- What have you learned about God's will for your life through sincere, intimate conversation with God in prayer?

- When, if ever, are you afraid to let God into your heart?

Warm-up: Categorize

What You'll Need

a list of categories (described below)

For this game, youth need to be standing up and mingling. While the youth are mingling, call out a category and have the youth divide into groups according to that category. For example, you might say, "Eye color." The youth with brown eyes would find one another and form a group, the blue-eyed youth would form a group, the green-eyed youth would form a group, and so on. When the youth have successfully divided into groups (so that there is only one brown group, one hazel group, and so forth), call out another category. With each successive category, get more personal. Categories could include

- grade level or school,
- favorite color,
- number of siblings, and
- type of music they enjoy most.

After completing the game with additional categories that would work well with your group, ask:

- What did you learn about your fellow youth while playing this game?

- Which of the categories we used in this game revealed the most about you?

- What other categories would help you get to know one another better?

Teaching

Give this talk to the large group; or put it in your own words, using the key Scriptures and your own illustrations. Begin by updating the youth on what's going on in your youth ministry (PPT 2).

In the two previous units, we looked at several practices and behaviors that help us mature in our faith. We've talked about prayer, devotional reading, having relationships grounded in love and forgiveness, honoring our bodies, and cleaning out the junk in our lives. Through all these ways, we can connect and grow closer to God. But to truly grow in our relationship with God—to truly know God—we have to set our hearts and minds on the Lord. We can't just go through the motions.

Think about doing homework and studying for tests. What is your study environment like? Do you sit at a well-lit desk or table in a quiet room? Do you flop down on the couch and turn on the TV (PPT 3)?

Ask the youth to answer the questions about their study environment on their Message Map. Then instruct them to divide into pairs or groups of three and discuss their study environment. Give the youth a few minutes to discuss; then continue (PPT 4).

Certain people study well in certain environments, but some factors make effective studying difficult—even impossible. If you try doing homework while you're watching your favorite TV show, your work will probably be sloppy and you won't learn much from the assignment. If you study for a test while listening to loud music and stopping every five minutes to IM your friends, you probably won't retain much information the next day when your teacher hands out the test papers.

In other words, the amount of time you spend studying isn't all that matters. If your mind isn't focused on your studies, you won't have a firm grasp on what you're studying. If your heart isn't in it, you may memorize some key points but you won't truly understand what they mean.

The same goes with practicing our faith. The number of hours each week we spend in prayer, at church, or in service to others doesn't tell the whole story. If we do these things only to make ourselves feel better or to cross them off a to-do list, we miss an opportunity to grow closer to God.

The unit we're starting today deals with calling. Over the next few sessions, we'll look at how God calls out to us and how we should respond.

Today we're looking at how we're called to know God. We can respond to this call in several ways. First, we can respond by being **religious** (PPT 5). For the most part, being religious is a good thing. It's good to spend time praying, reading Scripture, attending worship, and being active in our congregation. The danger in being religious comes when we start congratulating ourselves for all of the ways we worship and express devotion to God. Developing spiritual habits is important; but we need to do so for God's glory, not our own.

Give the youth a minute to answer the question on their Message Map about being religious.

Secondly, we can respond by becoming a **brainiac** (PPT 6). When we experience God's love, we want to learn more about God. We learn about God by reading and studying Scripture, going to Sunday school, and participating in Bible study. While God doesn't ask us all to become Bible-trivia champions, God does want us to know the story of God and God's people. The Bible not only offers guidance on how to live but also tells us about who the Lord is and how the Father relates to us. Of course, we need to remember that a difference exists between knowing God and knowing *about* God. When we open our Bibles, we shouldn't just sit down and read; instead, we need to open ourselves to the Lord and allow God to speak to us through Scripture.

Give the youth a minute to answer the question on their Message Maps about being a brainiac. Ask for volunteers to read aloud their answers.

Another answer to God's call is the **goodie-goodie** response (PPT 7). Again, being good—being righteous—is an important part of our faith, and God's love should inspire us to be good people. The Book of James even tells us that without good works, our faith is dead. But this relationship between faith and works goes both ways. If we truly want to know God, our good deeds have to be an expression of our faith. Good works don't earn us points for salvation; they are a response to God's love and grace.

Give the youth a minute to answer the question on their Message Map about being goodie-goodie. Ask for volunteers to read aloud their answers.

Finally we can respond to the call to know God by **name checking** (PPT 8). As Christians, we profess that we are children of God and followers of Christ. But if we invoke God's name and claim to be disciples of Christ, we have to back it up. Let's look at **Matthew 7:22-23.** (PPT 9).

*Read aloud **Matthew 7:22-23** while the youth follow along.*

Calling ourselves Christians or saying that we know God isn't enough. We need to listen to God and to follow Jesus' teachings. Only then can we truly know God.

Give the youth a minute to answer the question on their Message Map about name checking. Instruct the youth to divide into pairs or groups of three to discuss their answers.

We are called to know God. Think about the people you know the best, such as friends, parents, siblings, and people at church. Chances are that you spend a lot of time with these people, you've been to their homes (or live with them), you eat meals with them, and you do activities with them. But you can spend time with a person without truly getting to know him or her. If you want to know someone and vice versa, you have to open up. You have to talk to that person about likes and dislikes, highs and lows, successes and failures. You have to listen to, pay attention to, and care about that person.

The same goes for God. If we truly want to know the Lord, we need to open ourselves to God, talk with God about our joys and worries, to listen to God, and to pay attention to how God is working in our lives.

To close I want to read a covenant that God made with God's chosen people in the Book of Jeremiah (PPT 10).

*Read aloud **Jeremiah 31:33-34a:***

> This is the covenant that I will make with the house of Israel after those days, says the Lord: I will put my law within them, and I will write it on their hearts; and I will be their God, and they shall be my people. No longer shall they teach one another, or say to each other, "Know the Lord," for they shall all know me, from the least of them to the greatest.

God knows each one of us and wants to be known by us. We can all know God because God dwells within us. We just need to open our minds and hearts to God, to listen to what God says, and to give ourselves fully to God (PPT 11).

Let's pray.

> God, we want to know you more fully. Give us the courage to get to know you better through worship, Scripture, fellowship, and all of the blessings you've given us. Help us also to get to know you better by being faithful to your teachings and commandments. In Jesus' name we pray. Amen.

The Call: You Are Here

The Big Idea

To use a map effectively, we must fist know where we are. Without that key piece of information, any map is useless. Likewise, to answer God's call, we must be able to identify where we are so that we can better understand where we need to go. We can map our spiritual maturity by defining four stages of development: seeker, believer, follower, and reproducer.

Session Texts

- **Matthew 28:19-20** (NRSV): "Go therefore and make disciples of all nations, baptizing them in the name of the Father and of the Son and of the Holy Spirit, and teaching them to obey everything that I have commanded you. And remember, I am with you always, to the end of the age."

- **Acts 8:30-31** (NRSV): Philip ran up to [the chariot] and heard [the Ethiopian] reading the prophet Isaiah. He asked, "Do you understand what you are reading?" He replied, "How can I, unless someone guides me?" And he invited Philip to get in and sit beside him.

- **Hebrews 6:1** (*Message*): So come on, let's leave the preschool fingerpainting exercises on Christ and get on with the grand work of art. Grow up in Christ. The basic foundational truths are in place: turning your back on "salvation by self-help" and turning in trust toward God; baptismal instructions; laying on of hands; resurrection of the dead; eternal judgment. God helping us, we'll stay true to all that. But there's so much more. Let's get on with it!

Before You Teach This Lesson

Where are you on your spiritual journey? Where have you come from? Where are you headed?

You cannot help guide your youth along the path of discipleship without traveling that path yourself. Read through this lesson and the descriptions of "seeker," "believer," "follower," and "reproducer." Think about which of these stages of the journey fits you best. Think back on when in your life have you advanced from one stage to the next. What enabled you to take that next step?

e|Merge 1.0: Director's Guide

Think through these questions as you prepare to teach this lesson:

- When did your Christian journey begin? How did God lead you down the path toward Christian discipleship before you even knew that path existed?

- In what ways does God lead you (or push you) toward a more fulfilling life in Christ?

- If you had only one hour to express to your students the meaning of walking the path of Christian discipleship, what would you say?

Warm-up: Where Are You Going?

> **What You'll Need**
> a blindfold

Select one volunteer, and ask this person to leave the room and put on a blindfold. Bring this volunteer back into the room, spin this person around several times, and place him or her somewhere in the middle of the room. Then instruct the blindfolded youth to travel to a certain destination within the room, such as the door, a window, or a table. If the teen has trouble getting to the destination, allow him or her to ask three yes-or-no questions about where he or she is in the room. Repeat this activity with other volunteers as time permits; then discuss the game.

Ask the volunteers who were blindfolded:

- How long did you take to get a good idea of where you were in the room?

- What did you do to figure out where you were and where you needed to go?

Ask all of the youth:

- When you go on a trip, how do you figure out where you are at any given moment? *(a map, familiar landmarks, and so on)*

- What do you need to know to reach your destination? *(where you are currently, what roads or paths will take you from where you are to your destination, and so on)*

Teaching

Give this talk to the large group; or put it in your own words, using the key Scriptures and your own illustrations. Begin by updating the youth on what's going on in your youth ministry (PPT 2).

Many journeys are broken up into stages. A family might break up a vacation into two days at the Grand Canyon, three days in the Colorado Rockies, four days at Yellowstone National Park, and two days to get home. People who travel overseas for vacation, mission work, or business may have to go through several stages just to reach their first destination. Musicians who travel may have gigs in twenty-or-so cities, staying in each city for one or two days before moving on to the next stop.

The unit we're doing right now looks at God's call (PPT 1). Today we're going to talk about how God calls us to advance along the stages of our spiritual journey. We're going to focus on four main stages of spiritual growth and how God leads us and guides us through these stages.

But to start, I want to ask, How many of you have cell phones (PPT 3)?

Ask the youth to answer the question by raising their hands.

If you have a cell phone, you probably enjoy using it to text-message and talk to your friends. Your parents, on the other hand, may have other reasons for wanting you to have a phone. Your parents know that if you ever get in trouble, get lost, or get stuck somewhere (especially if you drive), you can give them a call and get help, directions, or a ride home.

Mobile phones have become an important asset for many people who travel. Without having to worry about pay phones or calling cards, travelers can use cell phones to connect with people at home, check on flights and hotel reservations, or order food. Just as these travelers keep their cell phones handy, spiritual travelers need to be prepared at any stage in their journey to answer God's call or to call on God for guidance.

Let's look at the stages of our spiritual journey and how we can connect with God at each stage.

e|Merge 1.0: Director's Guide

We begin our journey as **seekers** (PPT 4). A seeker may not know anything about God or the life, death, and resurrection of Christ. A seeker may not be fully aware of how God is already at work in his or her life. But seekers do have a sense that there is something more—that their lives are part of something much bigger. A seeker may visit several churches, research various faith traditions, and ask tough questions about God in hopes of finding meaning.

(If you claim a Wesleyan heritage, you might describe a seeker as someone who experiences God's prevenient grace.)

Do you consider yourself a seeker (PPT 5)? If not, do you remember a time when you were a seeker? Take a minute to answer the question on your Message Map about being a seeker.

*Give the students a few minutes to work; then read aloud **Acts 2:26-37** (PPT 6) and invite the students to follow along.*

The Ethiopian in this Scripture is a seeker. He knows that God is working to save and redeem the world, but he doesn't understand how. God works through the apostle Philip to teach the Ethiopian about Christ. When the Ethiopian learns about the good news of Christ, he goes from being a seeker to being a **believer** (PPT 7).

Believers profess the Christian faith. A believer knows about Christ and understands that Christ died and rose from the dead to defeat sin and death. Some Christians, when they become believers, get baptized. Others who were baptized as infants or children may go through confirmation or catechism to profess their faith in Christ and learn more about what being a Christian means. Baptism and confirmation are ways God calls out to us, inviting us to believe, and ways we call back to God saying, "Yes, I believe."

(If you claim a Wesleyan heritage, you might describe a believer as someone who experiences God's justifying grace.)

Are you a believer (PPT 8)? What beliefs do you profess? If you're not a believer, what questions do you have about the Christian faith? Take a minute to answer the questions on your Message Map about being a believer.

Give the students a few minutes to work on their Message Map.

The Call: You Are Here   77

Our Christian journey doesn't end with belief. Believing is only one stage of the journey (PPT 9).

*Read aloud **Hebrews 6:1-3** (Message).*

The author of Hebrews warns us not to get stuck but to keep growing in faith—to continue on our journey. As we continue to mature in faith, we become **followers** (PPT 10). As the word suggests, followers follow Christ. They not only believe in Jesus but also work to obey his teaching. Followers develop spiritual disciplines such as prayer, Scripture reading, and acts of mercy and justice that draw them closer to God. A follower checks in with God consistently, not just when he or she is lost or in trouble.

(If you claim a Wesleyan heritage, you might describe both followers and reproducers as persons who experience God's sanctifying grace.)

Are you a follower (PPT 11)? If so, how have you been able to turn belief into action? How do you live out your faith on a daily basis? If not, what spiritual habits can you develop that will take you from being a seeker or believer to being a follower? Take a minute to answer the questions on your Message Map about being a follower.

Give the students a couple minutes to work on their Message Map.

While a Christian should never stop being a believer or a follower, we can all go one step further along our journey by becoming a **reproducer** (PPT 12).

*Read aloud **Matthew 28:19-20** (PPT 13).*

Christ calls us to call others. As Christians, we have an important and life-saving message to tell others. When we become followers, we should be compelled to help others become followers. We should "reproduce" followers of Christ. We do so by telling our stories of faith, inviting others into our youth group and congregation, and showing people by our example how Christ transforms lives. As reproducers, we communicate not only with God but also with people.

How can you tell your story of faith to others and bring others closer to Christ? On your Message Map, answer the question about being a reproducer.

Give the students a couple minutes to work on their Message Map.

No matter where you are on the journey, the Lord is calling to you (PPT 14), inviting you to take the next step. And if you go astray or get bogged down by distractions, you can always get on the phone and call God, and the Lord will guide you back to the right path.

Let's pray.

> Lord, our guide, watch over us as we travel along the path that you have set before us. Help us as we take the next step on our journey, and help us to stay focused on our destination. Amen.

The Call: Can You Hear Me Now?

The Big Idea

Even the most devout, faithful Christians go through times when God seems distant and prayers seem to go unanswered. But God is always present, even in the most dire circumstances. Through worship, we can become more aware of how God's Holy Spirit is at work in our midst.

Session Texts

• **Numbers 14:1-3:** Then all the congregation raised a loud cry, and the people wept that night. And all the Israelites complained against Moses and Aaron; the whole congregation said to them, "Would that we had died in the land of Egypt! Or would that we had died in this wilderness! Why is the Lord bringing us into this land to fall by the sword? Our wives and our little ones will become booty; would it not be better for us to go back to Egypt?"

• **Deuteronomy 8:10-14:** You shall eat your fill and bless the LORD your God for the good land that [God] has given you.

Take care that you do not forget the LORD your God, by failing to keep [God's] commandments, [God's] ordinances, and [God's] statutes, which I am commanding you today. When you have eaten your fill and have built fine houses and live in them, and when your herds and flocks have multiplied, and your silver and gold is multiplied, and all that you have is multiplied, then do not exalt yourself, forgetting the LORD your God, who brought you out of the land of Egypt, out of the house of slavery.

• **John 4:23:** The hour is coming, and is now here, when the true worshipers will worship the Father in spirit and truth, for the Father seeks such as these to worship [God].

Before You Teach This Lesson

How do you worship, thank, and praise God? Do you say prayers of thanksgiving before meals, or at times when you especially sense God's presence? Do you give glory to God when you do the things you love (whether they be sports, music, enjoying nature, or something else)?

Think through these questions as you prepare to teach this lesson:

• How does your congregation worship? What elements of worship appeal most to you?

• What about God's love most compels you to respond in worship?

• For what do you give thanks to God? How do you express your thanks?

• If you had only one hour to express to your students how to respond to God's call through worship, what would you say?

Warm-up: Matching Tunes

Beforehand, think of several hymns and praise songs that will be familiar to most of your youth. Write each song title on two cards.

> **What You'll Need**
> one index card per youth,
> hymnals or songbooks
> (optional)

Place the cards face down on a table or the floor. Instruct the youth to select a card then spread out throughout the room. When you say, "Go," the youth should walk around the room singing or humming the song on the card they drew. The goal is for each youth to find the other person who is singing or humming his or her song.

(Hymnals or songbooks will be helpful in case some of the youth are new to the church and unfamiliar with the songs on the cards. Even if these youth can't figure out the tune of the songs, they will be able to speak the lyrics or sing the lyrics to a different tune.)

When you are finished, ask:

• What was most challenging about this activity? How difficult was it to find the other person singing your song?

• Why, do you think, are songs such an important part of most worship services?

• How do sacred songs and other forms of worship help you focus more intently on God?

Teaching

Give this talk to the large group; or put it in your own words, using the key Scriptures and your own illustrations. Begin by updating the youth on what's going on in your youth ministry (PPT 2).

A few years back, a wireless phone company launched an advertising campaign built around the question, "Can you hear me now?" (PPT 3). The purpose was to tell consumers that no matter where they went, they would be able to pick up a clear signal on their brand of phone.

Can you hear me now? is a question that God has probably asked each of us on several occasions, and we've discussed in previous sessions the importance of listening to God. But sometimes we find ourselves asking God the same question: "God, can you hear me now?" Sometimes, particularly during times of crisis, the Lord seems distant and we wonder whether God is truly listening to our prayers.

Wondering whether God is listening or is out there at all is a natural response when life gets rough and we feel alone. Most of us, at one time or another, have questioned God's ways. But we can't let doubt and despair become a way of life. We need to keep calling to God in times when we have trouble hearing God's response. One important way we call God is through worship.

Since the beginning, worship has been an important part of God's relationship with God's people. For the ancient Israelites, worship was a reminder that they were dependent on the Father for their survival and well-being. The Israelites participated in an array of rituals, praising and thanking God for food, water, safety, and the laws that shaped the community.

*Read aloud **Deuteronomy 8:10-14** (PPT 4, 5).*

God, through Moses, warns the people of Israel not to take credit for food, health, or prosperity but to give credit to God. Of course, this commandment is easier to follow when things are going well than when things are going badly. On several occasions, the Israelites became so overwhelmed by their struggles and frustrations that they lost sight of all that the Lord had done for them and they turned from God or rebelled against God.

One example of this defiance comes from the Book of Numbers (PPT 6). In this Scripture, Israelite spies have discovered that God is leading the people into a land occupied by giant warriors. Instead of trusting God to deliver them, the people got fussy.

*Read aloud **Numbers 14:1-3.***

Message Map (on the DVD)

We can easily look back on the Israelites and criticize them for turning their back on God. But are we truly any different? Think of a time (or times) when you have doubted God or forgotten about God (PPT 7). Write about this time on your Message Map.

Questioning and getting frustrated with God is just part of being human. But I want to challenge you to keep worshiping God during these difficult times of doubt. Worship is a way we can say to God, "Can you hear me now?" And as we worship, God's response to us will become clearer. The question now is, What is worship? (PPT 8). On your Message Map, write between five and ten words that come to mind when you think of worship.

Invite the youth to call out some of the words they wrote down.

Worship takes place in many styles and settings. Some congregations worship with traditional hymns and prayers; some prefer guitars, drums, and visuals projected on a big screen; still, others worship silently in spaces dimly lit by candles. Worship can be planned, such a service every Sunday at 11:00. It can also be spontaneous, such as a group of people singing songs to God around a campfire. Worship usually takes place in a community of people who love and support one another (PPT 9). Think about how you worship, and record your reflections on your Message Map.

Invite volunteers to read aloud what they have written.

No matter how you give praise and thanksgiving, worship needs to be an integral part of your life. You need to find ways to worship even when it's the last thing you want to do. Jesus tells us that as believers, we are supposed to worship God (PPT 10).

*Read aloud **John 4:23.***

We don't always feel like worshiping; sometimes we may not even feel like God is present (PPT 11). But worship is an important and effective way for us to connect with God—especially when we're struggling with doubt and despair.

Let's pray.

> God, thank you for the opportunity to grow closer to you through worship. We confess that we don't give you the praise that you deserve and that we don't always worship you with our whole hearts and minds. Help us to focus on you and connect with you during worship and to find ways to worship you even when we go forth from this place. Amen.

The Call: Keeping the Lines Clear

The Big Idea

The realm of communication has four major players: the sender, the receiver, the message, and the noise. In our conversations with God, we need to eliminate the noise so that we can accurately and consistently hear God's voice.

Session Texts

• **1 Samuel 3:1-10** (*Message*): The boy Samuel was serving God under Eli's direction. This was at a time when the revelation of God was rarely heard or seen. One night Eli was sound asleep (his eyesight was very bad—he could hardly see). It was well before dawn; the sanctuary lamp was still burning. Samuel was still in bed in the Temple of God, where the Chest of God rested.

Then God called out, "Samuel, Samuel!"

Samuel answered, "Yes? I'm here." Then he ran to Eli saying, "I heard you call. Here I am."

Eli said, "I didn't call you. Go back to bed." And so he did.

God called again, "Samuel, Samuel!"

Samuel got up and went to Eli, "I heard you call. Here I am."

Again Eli said, "Son, I didn't call you. Go back to bed." (This all happened before Samuel knew God for himself. It was before the revelation of God had been given to him personally.)

God called again, "Samuel!"—the third time! Yet again Samuel got up and went to Eli, "Yes? I heard you call me. Here I am."

That's when it dawned on Eli that God was calling the boy. So Eli directed Samuel, "Go back and lie down. If the voice calls again, say, 'Speak, God. I'm your servant, ready to listen.'" Samuel returned to his bed.

Then God came and stood before him exactly as before, calling out, "Samuel! Samuel!"

Samuel answered, "Speak. I'm your servant, ready to listen."

- **1 Kings 19:11-13** (*Message*): Then [Elijah] was told, "Go, stand on the mountain at attention before God. God will pass by."

A hurricane wind ripped through the mountains and shattered the rocks before God, but God wasn't to be found in the wind; after the wind an earthquake, but God wasn't in the earthquake; and after the earthquake fire, but God wasn't in the fire; and after the fire a gentle and quiet whisper.

When Elijah heard the quiet voice, he muffled his face with his great cloak, went to the mouth of the cave, and stood there. A quiet voice asked, "So Elijah, now tell me, what are you doing here?"

- **Isaiah 30:21** (NRSV): When you turn to the right or when you turn to the left, your ears shall hear a word behind you, saying, "This is the way; walk in it."

Before You Teach This Lesson

Think about what God has called you to do in your life. When have you eagerly responded to God's call? When have you run away from it? When have you had trouble figuring out what God was saying to you?

Listening to the Lord can be difficult, especially if we don't make prayer a habit. We are inundated with noise that makes focusing on God's voice a challenge. Noise may come in the form of pride, greed, or stress. To grow in our relationship with God, we need to find ways to shut out the noise and keep the lines clear.

Think about these questions as you prepare to teach this lesson:

- When you pray, how much difficulty do you have focusing on God? What "noise" distracts you when you pray?

- What interests or obsessions distract you from your bond with God? How do they keep you from fully obeying God's will for your life?

- How much effort do you put into listening to God? What practices help you focus on God's voice?

- If you had only one hour to teach your students about blocking out the noise and focusing on God's voice, what would you say?

Warm-up: Crossed Lines

Divide the group into teams of six or eight. Tell each team to gather in a circle. In the middle of each circle, set out one rope for every two youth. Have each youth hold one end of one rope so

> **What You'll Need**
> a six-foot piece of rope per two students (which are available at hardware stores or at *esportsonline.com*)

that all of the ropes cross in the middle of the circle. Then instruct the youth to spend about thirty seconds moving over and under one another's ropes, tangling and knotting the ropes.

After the youth have had a chance to create their tangled web, challenge the teams to untangle their ropes. Give them a few minutes to work.

As time permits, try this activity several times. If you have multiple groups, have the students switch groups each time you play.

Teaching

Give this talk to the large group; or put it in your own words, using the key Scriptures and your own illustrations. Begin by updating the youth on what's going on in your youth ministry (PPT 2).

Communication has four factors: the sender, the receiver, the message, and noise. When you talk to one of your friends on the phone, you are the sender, your friend is the receiver, the message is whatever you are chatting about, and the noise would include static and people talking in the background.

When you're in class, your teacher is the sender, you are the receiver, the message is the lesson, and the noise includes any notes passed to you by your friends or anything that you're daydreaming about.

Let's practice.

Instruct the youth to divide into pairs or groups of three.

Think of one way you communicate to others or others communicate with you. It can be at home, at school, at church, with your friends, or anywhere else you can think of (PPT 3). Then tell your group or partner about the situation you're thinking of. Who is the sender? Who is the receiver? What is the message? What is the noise?

The Call: Keeping the Lines Clear

Give the students a few minutes to discuss; then allow volunteers to talk about their communication scenarios.

We can also use these four factors—sender, receiver, message, and noise—to describe our communication with God. We communicate with God through prayer, through worship, and by keeping our minds and hearts open for God's voice. We're going to look at each of these factors, particularly the noise.

Ideally, communication with God should be a two-way conversation. God speaks to us in a variety of ways; and we should take our praises, concerns, and questions to the Father. Take a minute and list on your Message Maps ways you communicate with God, as well as ways the Lord communicates to you.

Give the youth a minute to write on their Message Maps.

Examples of ways we communicate with God include personal prayer, communal prayer, sacred songs, and liturgical dance. Examples of ways God communicates with us include warming our hearts, planting ideas in our minds, speaking to us through others, and putting us in situations that inspire us or give us clarity.

When we approach God through prayer and worship, God becomes our receiver. Likewise, when God speaks to us, we are the receivers. The story of how the Lord called the prophet Samuel illustrates what being a receiver means (PPT 4–7).

*Read aloud, or invite a youth to read aloud, **1 Samuel 3:1-10** from the slides or from a personal Bible.*

Samuel could hear God's voice, but he didn't become an effective receiver until he recognized that the voice was from God.

You've written about the ways God communicates to you, but how do you receive those messages (PPT 8)? How do you know whether a message or voice is actually from God? On your Message Map, write about receiving God's messages.

Give youth a minute to write on their Message Maps.

All this talk about senders and receivers is meaningless if there isn't a message. God doesn't speak gibberish to us, and we shouldn't babble about nothing to God. We have a lot of important messages to communicate to the Father: praise and thanksgiving, prayers of petition, requests to respond to our needs and the needs of others, and requests for for strength and guidance.

God also has important messages for us. God called Moses to free the Israelites from captivity in Egypt. God called Gideon to take on the Midianites. God called Esther to save her people from genocide. God called Paul to preach the gospel to the Gentiles. And the Lord has continued to call people throughout history. Sometimes, as with God's messages to biblical heroes, God clearly calls us to take on a major task. Often, however, the message is more subtle (PPT 9).

Read aloud, or ask a youth to read aloud, **Isaiah 30:21.**

God's message may be just a word of comfort and affirmation: "I am with you," or "Yes, you are headed in the right direction."

What messages has God communicated to you? On your Message Map, write about God's messages to you.

Give youth a minute to write on their Message Maps.

The final factor in our communication with God is noise. Noise includes everything that distracts us from our conversations with our Father and keeps us from listening to God's voice. Noise may include actual noise; have you ever tried praying in a crowded room where people are talking at full volume or while sitting at the corner of a busy intersection? It can be difficult. I'm not saying that you shouldn't pray in these settings, but staying focused can be tough. Even if you pray in noisy environments, you should also set aside time in a quiet space to go to God in prayer.

But noise is more than just loud and annoying sounds. Sometimes we have trouble focusing on worship or prayer because we're worried about a test, a game, or a fight we had with a friend. Instead of dwelling on these concerns and allowing them to distract us, we need to place these worries before God and make them a part of our prayer. The same goes for things that excite us. We may be tempted to rush through a prayer so that we can hurry up and listen to some new music we downloaded, eat a delicious meal, or call our friends to tell them some exciting news. But no matter how eager we are, we need to be patient and take time to thank God for these blessings that God has placed before us.

Write on your Message Map some of the joys and worries that become "noise" when you're worshiping or praying to God.

Give the youth a minute to write on their Message Maps. You might instruct the students to divide into pairs or groups of three and have them discuss the noise they wrote about.

Noise is a problem when we're talking to God; it's also a big problem when God is talking to us. Two common forms of noise that keep us from hearing God are pride and greed. When we take too much credit for the blessings in our lives, we shut out God and often do not hear God's message about how we should use these blessings. And when we get caught up in our desires and possessions, we overlook the Lord's promises to sustain us and provide for us and miss out on what God wants us to focus on. To break through the noises of pride and greed, we need to remind ourselves that we are not the center of the universe—God is.

Greed and pride are only two forms of noise that keep us from hearing the Lord. Write on your Message Map some of the other noises that keep you from hearing God's voice (PPT 10).

Give the youth a minute to write on their Message Maps. You might instruct the students to divide into pairs or groups of three and have them discuss the noise they wrote about.

To communicate effectively, both the sender and the receiver need to cut through the noise so that the message is delivered clearly. The same is true of our conversations with God. We need to find ways to shut out distractions so that we can clearly talk to and listen to God.

Let's pray.

God, help us to cut through all of the noise that surrounds us so that we can focus on our conversations with you. Give us the patience and courage to bring our worries to you and praise you for all of the blessings in our lives. Help us also to keep our hearts and minds open so that we might hear your voice. Amen.

The Call: Called to Follow

The Big Idea

Christ is calling us to follow him. This commitment involves risking everything. It means that our life is no longer our own. Christ has commissioned us to a life of ministry in which everything we do is directed toward God's mission on earth.

Session Texts

- **Matthew 28:16-20** (*Message*): Meanwhile, the eleven disciples were on their way to Galilee, headed for the mountain Jesus had set for their reunion. The moment they saw him they worshiped him. Some, though, held back, not sure about worship, about risking themselves totally.

  Jesus, undeterred, went right ahead and gave his charge: "God authorized and commanded me to commission you: Go out and train everyone you meet, far and near, in this way of life, marking them by baptism in the threefold name: Father, Son, and Holy Spirit. Then instruct them in the practice of all I have commanded you. I'll be with you as you do this, day after day after day, right up to the end of the age."

- **Luke 9:57-62** (*Message*): On the road someone asked if he could go along. "I'll go with you, wherever," he said.

  Jesus was curt: "Are you ready to rough it? We're not staying in the best inns, you know."

  Jesus said to another, "Follow me."

  He said, "Certainly, but first excuse me for a couple of days, please. I have to make arrangements for my father's funeral."

  Jesus refused. "First things first. Your business is life, not death. And life is urgent: Announce God's kingdom!"

  Then another said, "I'm ready to follow you, Master, but first excuse me while I get things straightened out at home."

  Jesus said, "No procrastination. No backward looks. You can't put God's kingdom off till tomorrow. Seize the day."

Before You Teach This Lesson

Following Christ is not meant to be easy or comfortable. Often, living out our faith involves courage, sacrifice, and a willingness to set aside our interests. Jesus was up front with his followers about what discipleship required: giving our whole lives over to Christ and never looking back.

Dropping everything and responding to God's call can be difficult in a culture where many things compete for our time and attention. The Lord asks us to give ourselves fully to following Christ, and God doesn't want excuses. What do you need to do to commit more fully to a life of discipleship?

Read **Luke 9:57-62**; then reflect on the following questions:

• What stands out to you the most about this Scripture? What is most difficult for you about following this teaching of Jesus?

• What earthly commitments keep you from giving yourself fully to Christ?

Read **Matthew 28:16-20**; then reflect on the following questions:

• How do you respond to the Great Commission (verses 19-20a)?

• How can you challenge and equip your youth to "go therefore and make disciples"?

Warm-up: White Elephant

What You'll Need
items described to the right, gift boxes, wrapping paper, basket or other container

Beforehand, collect several weird, silly, and no-longer-used items from around your house or church building. Wrap these items as gifts. Number slips of paper from one to the total number of packages. If you have a small number of youth, have one package for each person; if you have a larger group, limit the number of participants to the number of packages. (Those youth who aren't playing can shout suggestions to the youth who are.)

Place the slips of paper in a basket or other container, and have each participant draw a number. Ask the person with number 1 to choose

e|Merge 1.0: Director's Guide

one of the packages. After that gift has been opened and shown to the group, the person with number 2 can either "steal" that gift from number 1 or choose an unopened package. The person with number 3 can either steal from number 1 or 2 or select a new gift. Whenever a participant has been robbed of a gift, he or she can steal a gift from another person or choose an unopened gift. (The players cannot steal a gift back from someone who has stolen from them.) Continue until every participant has had a chance to steal or open a gift. Finally, let number 1 steal someone else's gift.

After the gift exchange, ask the participants:

• Did you end up with the gift you wanted? If not, what gift would you have liked?

• How did you decide whether to steal a gift or take a chance on opening something else? When did you pass up something you liked in hopes of getting something better?

• When were you afraid that a gift that you liked would be taken from you?

Say: "Today's session deals with following Christ. Being a faithful follower of Jesus often involves sacrifice and giving up things we enjoy. It can be difficult, because we sometimes have trouble seeing all the of benefits of following Christ. But God assures us that when we devote ourselves to Jesus, we claim a gift that will never be taken from us."

Video: Emma

Show the video "Emma" from the DVD then have the youth divide into groups of four to five to discuss these questions:

> **What You'll Need**
> "Emma" film from the DVD, DVD player or computer and projector

• What do you think is most extraordinary about Emma's story?

• In what ways does Emma follow Jesus' teaching by using her birthday as an opportunity to help people who are less fortunate than she is?

• What can you learn from Emma about following Christ?

The Call: Called to Follow

Teaching

Give this talk to the large group; or put it in your own words, using the key Scriptures and your own illustrations. Begin by updating the youth on what's going on in your youth ministry (PPT 2).

In this unit, "The Call" (PPT 1), we've looked at how God communicates to us and how we respond to God. In some ways, God's call is unique to each person: God has given each one of us specific gifts and calls us to use these gifts in specific ways. But in other ways, the Lord's call is universal. We are all called to be followers, or disciples, of Christ. Today, we're going to talk about responding to that call of discipleship (PPT 3).

What does following Jesus mean to you? What does it involve? Find one or more persons, and discuss the ways you follow Christ.

Give the youth a few minutes to discuss. You might offer suggestions such as "attending worship," "spending time in prayer and devotion," or "changing your attitude toward people different from you."

Which of these ways of following Christ are easy and comfortable? Which are difficult and require you to make sacrifices?

Give the youth another minute to discuss these questions.

Jesus taught, "Whoever does not carry the cross and follow me cannot be my disciple" (**Luke 14:27,** NRSV). In other words, true disciples must be willing to give their lives if it comes to that. Those of us who live in North America in the twenty-first century generally don't have to worry about dying for our faith; but many people throughout history and around the world today have risked their lives on behalf of their faith in Christ or their belief in principles such as mercy and justice.

Although we don't have to worry much about persecution, living a true life of faith can be quite a challenge. Jesus tells us that we need to be willing to set aside all earthly commitments and follow him (PPTs 4–5).

*Read aloud, or invite a youth to read aloud, **Luke 9:57-62.***

This teaching may seem shocking to you, and it was certainly shocking to some of the people who heard it first. I want you to think about this Scripture then answer the related questions on your Message Map

94   e|Merge 1.0: Director's Guide

(PPT 6). What do you find most shocking or difficult about this Scripture? What earthly commitments keep you from giving yourself more fully to Christ?

Give the youth a minute to answer these questions on their Message Maps.

Jesus isn't saying that our lives, work, friends, and family aren't important. These things are very important. But Christ comes first (PPT 7). Jesus teaches in his Sermon on the Mount, "Strive first for the kingdom of God and [God's] righteousness, and all these things will be given to you as well" (**Matthew 6:33,** NRSV). In other words, if we give our lives to Christ, we can trust that he will guide us and help us through all of the other challenges that arise.

So we know that following Christ is important. But what does it mean? For one, it means following Jesus' teaching. In Matthew, Jesus says, "Not everyone who says to me, 'Lord, Lord,' will enter the kingdom of heaven, but only the one who does the will of my Father in heaven" (**Matthew 7:21,** NRSV). Jesus, in the Gospels, gives us instructions for living in relationship with one another, for praying to and worshiping God, and for using our money and other resources

More specifically, after Jesus rose from the dead, and before he ascended to heaven, he gave all his followers an assignment. In the church we call it "The Great Commission" (PPTs 8–9).

*Read aloud, or invite a youth to read aloud, **Matthew 28:16-20.***

Jesus tells us not to keep our faith to ourselves. If we want to be true disciples, we need to help others become disciples. We do so by becoming a living witness to Christ's love, mercy, and salvation.

Following Jesus isn't about just being good. It's about living in a way that gives people hope and that transforms the world in a positive way. When people see how we as Christians express Christ's love, they too will be drawn to him.

We also witness to others through sacrifice. Giving of ourselves for others and honoring God by giving up certain behaviors may seem like a turn-off at first, but many people want to devote their lives to something meaningful. When you spend Sunday mornings in worship, evenings in fellowship with other Christians, weekends on retreats or service projects, and entire weeks over the summer at church camp or on mission trips, you show the world that your faith is worth your time, your money, your energy, and your talents. When people see that you are loving and compassionate, they will become aware of the power of Christ to transform lives (PPT 10).

Take a minute and list on your Message Map some ways people can see Christ at work in your life. This list is personal, so you don't have to show it to anyone.

Give the youth a minute to answer these questions on their Message Maps.

How do others know that you are a follower of Christ? How can you change your attitudes and behaviors so that others will be more aware of how Christ is at work in your life?

Before we close, I want to stress that following Christ and inviting others to follow Christ are not things that we do on our own. The Holy Spirit works in our minds and hearts and in the minds and hearts of others. We're just helping out. So don't get frustrated if you struggle to grow spiritually or if your message of faith seems lost on other people. Be patient, and trust the Holy Spirit (PPT 11).

Christian discipleship is a challenging, lifelong task that requires commitment and sacrifice. Discipleship also involves making disciples of others. We do so by becoming living witnesses to the power of Christ. And while Christian discipleship isn't easy, the Holy Spirit is always present to support us and guide us.

Let's pray.

> Eternal God, help us to give ourselves entirely to you and to become living witnesses to the gospel of Christ. Watch over us, especially when our faith challenges us and pushes us out of comfort zone. Give us the strength and patience to continue growing as disciples of Jesus Christ. Amen.